50 MEDITATIONS

50 MEDITATIONS

KOSUKE KOYAMA

ORBIS BOOKS

Maryknoll, New York 10545

1979

Second Printing, January 1983

Copyright © 1975 by Christian Journals Limited, 2 Bristow Park
Belfast BT9 6TH

All rights reserved

Typeset in Ireland by Cahill & Co., Dublin

Printed in the United States of America

Library of Congress Cataloging in Publication Data

Koyama, Kósuke, 1929-
    50 meditations.

    1.   Meditations.   I.   Title.
[BV4832.2.K68 1978]   242   77-7026
ISBN 0-88344-134-9 pbk.

CONTENTS

pilgrim or tourist

In Rangoon, Burma, the famous Shwe Dagon Pagoda stands on Singuttara Hill. It is an impressive monument. Its perimeter at the base is 1,476 feet. Its height is 344 feet. The octagonal base of the Pagoda is surrounded by 64 small pagodas. I have been there a few times. It was built, tradition says, to enshrine the Eight Sacred Hairs of the Buddha which the Buddha himself personally gave to the faithful visitors from Rangoon. The gold-gilded Pagoda is a marvel to view from nearby as well as from a distance. Visitors are required to remove their shoes and socks at the foot of the hill. ('... put off your shoes from your feet, for the place on which you are standing is holy ground.' Exodus 3:5) The approach itself is already in the sacred territory of the Sacred Eight Hairs. Every barefoot step prepares man to come into the presence of the holy.

The idea of baring one's feet is not in preparation for running. It shows respect and humility for the holy object which the devotee is approaching. There is an interesting story in the Hindu tradition. Krishna, an incarnation of Vishnu, stole the clothing of the shepherdesses while they were bathing. The maidens, realizing what happened and where their clothes were, cried for their clothes. Krishna told them that they must come and get them. The maidens, seeing no other way possible, came to Krishna wholly naked to retrieve their clothes. In this seemingly erotic story is hidden the rather impressive religious insight that man must not come to god 'covered up'. He must come to god 'naked'.

When I took off my shoes I felt that I was exposed. My modernized and well-protected feet found it hard to walk bare over gravel, stones and heated pavements. The acceptance of all this inconvenience, and in particular of the feeling of being exposed, forms the religious sense of humility and respect. Under the hot Rangoon sun I began to trudge up to the hill where the Pagoda stands. It was a slow climb. Every step was a ceremonially slow step. The sweat of my forehead was, as it were, religious sweat. The time I spent to walk up to the Pagoda was a holy time. When I arrived at the foot of the Pagoda itself, my mind was prepared to see it right in front of me. I recalled how in Japan the Meiji Emperor Shrine in Tokyo, Ise Imperial Grand Shrine in Mie Prefecture and a host of others have long approaches to the main shrine, some as long as a mile or more. No bicycles and no motor vehicles are allowed. Even the emperor himself must walk from a certain point. The holy must be approached slowly and carefully with respect and humility. The holy must not be approached by motorcycle or helicopter. It must be approached by walking.

Walking is the proper speed and the proper posture that can prepare man to meditate. Thus the universal use of the motor car is, I am afraid, producing a less-meditative mankind! The un-holy (everyday things) may be approached by running or on motorcycle (even if the silencer is broken). But that which is holy must be approached slowly. Such thoughts came to me as I was walking up to the Pagoda.

The God that the Bible proclaims reveals himself to be the holy God. He revealed himself to be holy by becoming *slow* for us. The central affirmation of the Bible is that God does not forsake man.

> Can a woman forget her suckling child, that she should have no compassion on the son of her womb? Even these may forget, yet I will not forget you. Isaiah 49:15

> For a brief moment I forsook you, but with great compassion I will gather you. In overflowing wrath for a moment I hid my face from you, but with everlasting love I will have compassion on you. Isaiah 54:7,8

The whole Bible is a commentary to that one passage in the Book of Genesis: 'Where are you?' (3:9) *God in search of man!*

> What man of you, having a hundred sheep, if he has lost one of them, does not leave the ninety-nine in the wilderness, and go after the one which is lost, until he finds it? Luke 15:3,4

This is the *holy* search. In his holy search the holy God did not go on a motorcycle or by supersonic jet. He became *slow*, very slow. The crucifixion of Jesus Christ, the son of God, means that God went so slow that he became nailed down in his search of man. What speed can be slower than the dead stop

9

of being nailed down? If God revealed in such a way his holy character, man must approach him in the same manner.

On my second visit to Rangoon I found that in the meantime they had built a lift to the top of the hill where the Pagoda stands! Invasion of technology and speed! No longer a slow approach is necessary. Electric energy will put you instantly in front of the Pagoda of the Sacred Eight Hairs in a matter of fifteen seconds or so. No steps. No Sweat.

At the entrance to the lift on the ground level, however, there is a sign which says that shoes must be removed before entering. For the first time in my life I went in a lift barefooted. My shoes in my hands shouted at me that they must be worn on my feet. While I was feeling the strange sensation of suspension between becoming a pilgrim and becoming a tourist I reached the top. If I had walked up the hill barefoot, I would have been a pilgrim, and if I had kept my shoes on in the lift I would have been a tourist. But now I was neither pilgrim nor tourist! A strange sensation of temporary loss of self-identity swept over me.

The traditional way of *slow* approach has been disturbed by the massive impact of technology. The whole of Asia is disturbed and disrupted in this way today and perhaps so is the whole world. Technology is shaking our basic self-identity because it is disturbing our spiritual relationship with the holy. Today all kinds of 'lifts' are being built in front of the 'holy pagodas'. Singapore hotel lifts do not

10

give me this problem. A Hong Kong shopping-centre lift does not give me this problem. But the Shwe Dagon Pagoda lift does! The number of 'Shwe Dagon Pagoda lift' situations is increasing today all over the world.

Should we prepare to come to the presence of the holy 'on a motorcycle'? Should we train in a new style of relating ourselves to the holy? Am I old fashioned in speaking of 'the *slow* God'? What should be the relationship between technology and our relationship with the holy? Can technology be made a creative servant of the man who lives by the grace of the searching God?

god of abraham, isaac, jacob

God also said to Moses, 'Say this to the people of Israel,
"The Lord, the God of your fathers, the God of Abraham,
the God of Isaac, and the God of Jacob has sent me to you:"
This is my name for ever and thus I am to be remembered
throughout all generations.' Exodus 3:15

When God introduced himself he quoted three *human* names. Yes. Three human names. Why did he not quote three names of his holy angels to introduce himself? Abraham, Isaac and Jacob! These are three colourful names.

Abraham was once called Abram. He was called by God to go out from the city of Ur, the Mesopotamian moon-worshipping centre. By leaving this cultured city of Ur he was to become the 'father of a multitude of nations'. Abraham did not have an easy time. Food shortage in the promised land (!) forced him to go down to Egypt to survive. There he told the Egyptians that Sarah, his beautiful wife, was his sister. This got him into deep trouble. Later his son Isaac made the same mistake with his wife Rebekah.

12

Isaac means *laugh* because his mother Sarah laughed when the angel of the Lord told her that she would conceive a son in her old age. The Bible has this extraordinary scene of the birth of Esau and Jacob:

> And Isaac prayed to the Lord for his wife, because she was barren; and the Lord granted his prayer, and Rebekah his wife conceived. The children struggled together within her; and she said 'If it is thus, why do I live?'... When her days to be delivered were fulfilled, behold, there were twins in her womb. The first came forth red, all his body like a hairy mantle; so they called his name Esau. Afterward his brother came forth, and his hand had taken hold of Esau's heel; so his name was called Jacob. Genesis 25:21-26

In his old age, Isaac's mind was obviously not functioning well. He made a terribly upsetting, serious mistake in giving the major blessing to Jacob instead of Esau.

> ... So Jacob went near to Isaac his father, who felt him and said, 'the voice is Jacob's voice, but the hands are the hands of Esau...' Genesis 27:22

This whole scheme of deceiving Isaac began when Rebekah overheard (tapped telephone!) the conversation between Isaac and Esau. Actually, the line of the patriarch must be Abraham, Isaac and Esau. But Jacob's strategy, guided by Rebekah, changed this to Abraham, Isaac and Jacob!

The stories about the patriarchs, which are many, are human stories of belief and unbelief, strength and weakness, vision of faith and shortsightedness, humility and arrogance, reconciliation and conflict. They are absolutely fascinating stories pointing to the living reality of the God who rules over the his-

13

tory of man. All these stories are precisely meant to be there when God quoted these three names. Not just the inspiring parts of their life stories, but the whole of their lives are quoted in the solemn context of God's self-introduction.

The holy God introduces himself by quoting these three human names as though that were the only proper way to introduce himself. 'This is my name for ever and thus I am to be remembered throughout all generations'! This is the Gospel. Our human names are quoted in God's self-introduction. This is Good News. When our names are quoted in God's self-introduction, we ourselves are introduced in the most fundamental and profound way, the depth of which perhaps none of us will ever be able to understand.

something more

Recently I visited Tarus Theological School in Kupang, Timor, an eastern island of Indonesia. Tarus Theological School has fifty-five students and is located outside the city. As you enter you see many chickens because the school runs a poultry farm and students also breed chickens for their personal income. When I met the students I began my lecture by asking them:

What do you see when you see chickens?

Student A: When I see chickens I see eggs. I can sell them and make money. (good businessman! We need this kind in our church.)

Student B: When I see chickens I see God. God created chickens. He created them for us to eat. (A good theologian, and lover of 'fried chicken'. Of course he must study the meaning of this great word 'creation'.)

Student C: When I see chickens I see a good family life. A hen impresses me always as a

15

good mother who takes care of her chicks. (A good family man. He will practise family planning. He will make a good minister.)

Student D: When I see chickens I see the difference between man and animal. A chicken doesn't have understanding as I do. We are very superior to chickens. (A good philosopher.)

I continued: Splendid. We have found out so many interesting things (interesting to us, not to chickens, I mean) from which we can begin our *theological* discussion. We all see *something more* when we see a chicken. A chicken is not just a chicken. Rice is not just rice. The sun is not just the sun. Rain is not just rain. A house is not just a house. A water-buffalo is not just a waterbuffalo. Everything has *something more*. When we see chickens and see *only* chickens, then our life is dry and uninteresting. People do not come to us and listen to the message of Jesus Christ if we are 'dry and uninteresting' persons.

An interesting person means a person who always sees *something more* and is able to communicate *something more* to his neighbours. You are now studying theology. Theology, it seems to me, requires the mind to see *something more* in the ordinary things. Indeed, we must be able to see the power of the Creator himself in a chicken, even though a few hours later it will become 'fried chicken'. 'Now if God so clothes the flowers of the field, which are alive today and burnt in the stove

16

tomorrow...' (Matthew 6:30). This is the way Jesus saw *something more* in the wild flowers.

Will it not change our life if we have more and more of this kind of mind? The mind which sees an extraordinary message in an ordinary thing. Wait! What is an ordinary thing? Is there such a thing as an ordinary thing? Name one. Isn't everything amazingly extraordinary—for the 'extraordinary God' creates them and redeems them?

Students: Professor Small Mountain. We will look at chickens more carefully and eat them more carefully.

Right! Eat them carefully, taste them carefully.

> Whether you eat or drink, or whatever you are doing do all for the honour of God. I Corinthians 10:31

17

high-powered words

We must not say what we do not mean, particularly in relation to God. How very difficult that is! 'You shall not make wrong use of the name of the Lord your God.' (Exodus 20:7) Who among us can be free from this 'wrong use of the name of God'? We speak about God as easily as we speak of oranges and apples. If we speak of God to scare people they will hear only two or three times and no more. And we, ourselves, tend not to hear what we are saying after a time. The most dangerous aspect of this situation is that we do not believe what we ourselves are saying and even though we know that to be the case still we pretend to believe it. We are, as it were, hypnotized by our own beautiful and inspiring religious 'words'. We become irresponsible in our relation to God and neighbour through the careless use of 'many words'.

Yes, we use a lot of *high-powered* words, such as, 'love of God', 'Christ, the hope of the world', 'salvation from death', 'eternal salvation versus eternal damnation', 'hope against despair', and so on. These are, to use an image, very 'high-voltage' words. We must handle them with care lest we electrocute ourselves. Powers carelessly used destroy instead of serving.

Our church services are packed with high-voltage words. We sing:

Faith of our fathers, holy faith!
We will be true to thee till death.

When we sing this to organ accompaniment and with a hymn book in our hands, we feel exalted but do we *really* mean 'we will be true to death'? Do we mean what we say? Isn't Christianity simply too talkative, not so much in the sense of speaking a lot but using high-powered words irresponsibly?

beauty salon jesus

The New Testament does not give us any information about the physical appearance of Jesus, how
tall he was, the shape of his nose, the colour of his
eyes and hair. Did he have brown hair? Did he
have big strong shoulders? We have never found
out these things. The whole New Testament is
silent about them. But what about the Apostle
Peter? Peter was a fisherman. Naturally we assume
he must have been a strong, suntanned robust fellow. But who knows? Scholars have made some
conjectures (that's all they can do) about Paul on
the basis of II Corinthians 12:7 ('I was given a
sharp physical pain') and Galatians 4:13-14 ('As
you know, it was bodily illness that originally led
to my bringing you the Gospel, and you resisted
any temptation to show scorn or disgust at the
state of my body'), that the apostle might have had
epilepsy, or some offensive eye trouble, or even
malaria. But here again we do not really know
about Paul's appearance.

The centre of the New Testament message is found
in John 3:16 'God loved the world so much that he

gave his only Son'. Obviously, in order to communicate this love of God the New Testament writers felt no need to give a description of the physical appearance of Jesus of Nazareth. It is as though they are clearly telling us that the love of God can be perfectly communicated without our knowing how Jesus looked. Humanly speaking Jesus may have looked attractive, or he may have looked unattractive. We don't know. A photograph of Jesus is not needed for the Christian faith. The Bible does not speak of his appearance, but his deeds. We only know 'Christ bought us freedom from the curse of the law by becoming for our sake an accursed thing' (Galatians 3:13) says Paul. 'An accursed thing'! What a bold thing to say! What an 'ugly' remark to make about Jesus Christ! How did he look when he became 'an accursed thing'? The Gospel does not speak. But the entire story of his becoming 'an accursed thing' for our sake is the heart of the Gospel.

Every time I see the picture of Jesus—I hope you know the particular one to which I am referring—a beautifully groomed Jesus looking as if he has just stepped out of a beauty salon (and he is brunette!) —I am puzzled. This Jesus is a middle-class Western society bourgeois (with an income of £5,000 a year!). He does not look 'an accursed thing'!

We do not know what he looked like. We do know what he became for our sake.

i want to see jesus' eyes

I see young people walking on the streets of Singapore wearing sleeveless shirts with big designs of hearts and letters saying 'I love you'. I see young girls in trousers and on the side of them appears the word *love* attractively embroidered. *Love* is the word you see everywhere in Orchard Road in Singapore, Nathan Road in Hong Kong, Ginza Street in Tokyo. It is nice to see the word written in all possible and imaginative ways. I don't want to see young people walking in shirts which say 'I hate you'; 'I love you' is much better.

Love means, according to Webster's Dictionary:

1. a strong affection for or attachment or devotion to a person or persons.
2. a strong liking for or interest in something; as her *love* of acting.
3. a strong, usually passionate, affection for a person of the opposite sex.
4. the person who is the object of such an affection; a sweetheart; a lover.
5. sexual passion or its gratification.
6. Love—Cupid, or Eros as the god of love.
7. in tennis, a score of zero.

8. in theology, (a) God's benevolent concern for mankind; (b) man's devout attachment to God; (c) the feeling of benevolence and brotherhood that people should have for each other.

Love is real. We experience love. We are not cold stone. (I hope not!) We know what affection, attachment, liking, interest and passion mean. We experience them. *We live* means we experience these *strong* emotions. Let's take up *attachment* for instance. A baby, even a day old, instinctively attaches itself to the ground of its life, the mother. A small child cries if he loses sight of his mother, whether at home or in the supermarket. A young man feels a *strong* attachment to a girl whom he loves. Parents feel attachment to their children even after they have grown up. Love is, whether we are aware of it or not, the fundamental human experience.

But this fundamental experience of love is not so simple. Love is a power of incredible creativity indeed. But it may become sick. It may become confused. It may become misdirected. It may suffer paralysis. It may be hit by convulsion. Love has a high voltage, to use another image. The more intense love becomes, the higher its voltage. When a high-voltage situation becomes confused, it produces a high-voltage confusion. That a mother loves a child involves, perhaps, no problem. But when a mother loves child A more than child B, then immediately a serious problem arises. That a husband loves his wife may be a trouble-free situation. But if the wife suspects that actually he loves her only because of her wealthy background,

23

a serious dispute may take place between them. A woman who loves her man and discovers that he has another charming woman instantly experiences a revolution as her high-voltage love changes into a high-voltage jealousy.

That a mother loves her child involves, I said, *perhaps* no problem. I meant that even in such a 'simple' situation love cannot be free from problems with any certainty. There are unhealthy ways of loving a child. Sometimes a mother's love is expressed in such a strange way as to destroy the child's capacity for loving others. One person's love may smother the potentiality for love in another person's life. The ways of love within human hearts and in human relationships are the most mysterious and inevitable issues in our everyday life experience. Love can make a person genuinely happy. In a different context love can make a person genuinely despairing. Tragedy is, as you know, usually the reverse side of the work of love. A young man kills himself when his love is rejected or found to be impossible to realize.

I feel I know what love is. The Webster definition outlines what I already knew. I lecture on the Bible. I have read theological books on the subject of human love and divine love. I know what love means. Yet I must confess that I do not quite know what love is. The subject of love reminds me of Augustine's famous reflection on 'time'. He says he knows what *time* is until someone asks what it is. I experience healthy love and unhealthy love. I experience both healthy love and unhealthy love

24

mixed up and coming together to me. When I experience unhealthy love I see what healthy love can be. I should say I experience the *power* of love, just as I experience the power of electricity when I tune in my radio.

The power of love is tremendous both in creation and destruction. It is a living, real power. To be alive means to *keep* experiencing this power. To be dead means to become utterly insensitive to the working of the power of love. No one, then, will reach the other side of the power of love as long as he lives. Love is a fundamental human experience. It is *fundamental* in the sense that no human person is free from it. If anyone were to become free from the power of love, that person would become a monster.

Every time I feel intensely the reality of the power of love in my everyday life, I yearn to meet Jesus. Meet Jesus? Exactly. I want to see his *eyes*. I am not particularly interested to see his hair-do, his stature, his nose or his complexion. But I want to see his eyes. ('The eye is the lamp of the body. So, if your eye is sound, your whole body will be full of light; but if your eye is not sound, your whole body will be full of darkness. If then the light in you is darkness, how great is the darkness!' Matthew 6:22-23). I ask no theologians to stand by when I meet Jesus to give me a theological exposition about his eyes. In silence, I just want to see his eyes by myself. 'The eye is the lamp'. The lamp shines. I want to experience the light that comes from his eyes. Leave me alone. If I were granted this extraordinary experience, I would feel directly what holy divine love is, what the essence of such love is and what the mystery of the power of such love is. Such an experience would cast a great flood of light upon my understanding of the work of love.

> For now we see in a mirror dimly, but then face to face. Now I know in part; then I shall understand fully, even as I have been fully understood. I Corinthians 13:12

I do not expect to meet Jesus as his contemporaries did two thousand years ago. But I imagine that his eyes must be 'seeking-man' eyes. No spoken word is necessary. His eyes say 'Where are you?' (Genesis 3:9). Is this just a fanciful imagination? It is an imagination based on the Christian faith. Faith imagines. Is there more encouraging, hope-generating and reviving experience than to be met by the *eyes that seek you*? What a joy to see those seeking eyes if you are lonely or in trouble! You are found by him. You are sought by him. This conviction—to live with this conviction—is to live by the power of the love of God.

> And when Jesus heard it, he said to them, 'Those who are well have no need of a physician, but those who are sick; I came not to call the righteous, but sinners'. Mark 2:17

I want to see Jesus' eyes. *Profound love and profound eyes!*

i-need-you-i-wait-for-you

I spend a lot of time waiting in airport lounges. Once I waited at Port Moresby airport New Guinea for eight hours from midnight to morning. The airport was quiet and cool, I stretched out on a bench. I was waiting for an F27 Fokker to take me to Rabaul.

When you boil water for your tea, you must wait. When you want to buy a £25 suit, you most likely have to wait until your next pay day. When you go home from your work, you must wait for the bus to come. When you write to someone in Tokyo, you must wait for an answer. It may take ten days. The crowning wait in family life is perhaps that of an expectant mother waiting for the arrival of a baby. If we look at it this way, our everyday life is a chain of waiting. A chain of waiting means a chain of 'needing'.

We need all kinds of things. But we do not like waiting. Of course, we don't! Waiting means inefficiency in terms of the use of time (what a waste of time!) and consequently it causes within us psychological irritation. Who among us enjoys waiting for half an hour for a crowded bus to come on the streets of Singapore after a hard day's work? An efficient society is a society that eliminates unnecessary waiting as much as possible. Then our needs are met without waiting. This arrangement is called efficiency. The telephone is efficient. Just dial and you get the person on the line immediately. Wireless service has this quality too. A private car is waiting for you to be driven. Science-technology has eliminated a great deal of waiting. Japanese poultry farmers found that a certain kind of sound of falling water will make a chicken lay eggs twice a day. So they made an artificial waterfall near the hen runs. The egg industry cannot afford much waiting! As our life becomes more and more efficient, we are happily getting to be more and more free from waiting.

Waiting is irritating. Yet, it seems to me to be an essential part of human life. When I wait for my turn at the Vehicle Registration Office on Middle Road in Singapore, I am, in fact, recognizing one important factor in human life; 'I need your help' (in this case that of the person who represents the government and registers my car). *My life cannot be fulfilled simply by myself.* Hence I must wait.

Waiting, whether in the context of Vehicle Registration Office or the dentist's waiting room or the airport lounge, or children waiting for the return of their mother from shopping—waiting means 'I need you'. If 'I don't need you' why should I wait at all? As long as we live human life in human community 'waiting' is inevitable. And if waiting means 'I need you' it can be a beautiful experience! For young lovers every minute of waiting to see each other is an exciting and hopeful experience.

'I need you!'—this is the most inspiring thing one can say to someone. To say 'I need you!' to God is faith. But, as we have seen, 'I need you!' implies 'I wait for you'. Somehow we know from our life experience that 'I need you!' and 'I wait for you' are inseparably related. Christian faith is to live on the basis of this combination. 'I-need-you-I-wait-for-you'. Waiting is another name for faith.

person-message, message-person

In theology what do we study? We study the Bible carefully. We study its historical background, its religious and cultural world, and its languages. Since the Bible is not a Chinese or an Indonesian book (alas!) but a Semitic book written in entirely different historical and cultural times it takes a great deal of effort on our part to study it. Advanced students study the Old Testament in Hebrew and the New Testament in Greek. These languages are by no means easy to master. This however—even though it involves an immense area of study—is not the whole story of the study of theology.

We try to hear and understand the living message of the Bible for us today. What, for instance, is God saying through the Bible to us in Hong Kong or Jakarta today? Theology, then, is certainly not an antique study. In theology, the Bible must become for us the Asian Year Book.

How are we to know the message for Indonesians today communicated through the book which was written many centuries ago—culturally, religiously and historically—and far from Indonesia? This involves the science of interpretation which is necessary if we are to avoid dangerous (pious) 'guess work'. First we must understand what the Bible texts said to the people being addressed at that time. We find the message and we see how the people reacted. To say this, however, is not enough, since the message alone is not a message. It is only a message when it confronts us in Jesus Christ. Why? Because Jesus Christ is the message— in the message in person. He is a walking message. Jesus Christ is the Message-Person, Person-Message. They are inseparable in him. Look at this incident:

> On another sabbath, when he entered the synagogue and taught, a man was there whose right hand was withered. And the scribes and the Pharisees watched him, to see whether he would heal on the sabbath, so that they might find an accusation against him. But he knew their thoughts, and he said to the man who had the withered hand, 'Come and stand here.' And he rose and stood there. And Jesus said to them, 'I ask you, is it lawful on the sabbath to do good or to do harm, to save life or to destroy it?' And he looked around on them all, and said to him, 'Stretch out your hand.' And he did so, and his hand was restored. But they were filled with fury and discussed with one another what they might do to Jesus. Luke 6:6-11

Here Jesus confronts people with specific immediacy: 'Come and stand here!' '... is it lawful on the sabbath to do good or to do harm, to save life or to destroy it?' 'Stretch out your hand!' His word represents his Person. What he says comes from what he is. What he is is the whole content of his message. This Person-Message we must relate to Hong Kong and Indonesia today. We do not transport some

31

The *Word Person*
Jesus Christ

noble ideals or message over the gap of twenty centuries. We make the power of the Person-Message, Message-Person outstanding in Hong Kong. Is it true that He cannot be in Hong Kong unless we bring him? No! That he ascended into heaven means he is free from time and space. He, the Person-Message Message-Person, is in Hong Kong in spirit. Theology is a humble finger pointing to the presence of Jesus Christ through the thoughts and acts meaningful to the people of Hong Kong today.

renunciation-affirmation

No man can attain anything of value without discipline. For instance, only with concentrated effort and discipline is a man able to play an intricate piece of music on the piano or violin. Life without discipline lacks backbone—power to have a meaningful existence. All great religions call for a disciplined life. Discipline implies self-control. Self-control is seen to be a virtue. It is noble and heroic.

The New Testament, however, speaks of a radical kind of 'self-denial'. '... If any man would come after me, let him deny himself and take up his cross and follow me.' (Mark 8:34). This is more than self-control. It has a tone of a 'kamikase' (Japanese suicide plane in the last war) undertaking. 'Take up his cross' means man must be ready to accept death, and that is exactly the meaning of 'let him deny himself'. 'And follow me' opens a new dimension. That is to say, 'let him deny himself' is not a solitary act of spiritual and mental courage. It does not mean to become an individual as lonely as 'a wandering rhinoceros in the desert' as the

Buddhist text says. 'Let him deny himself' means to become part of a new community. This is the promised community made up of the people 'denying themselves'.

'Let him deny himself' is an act of freedom. One has the freedom to 'deny himself'. The community, the community of self-renunciation, as it were, is a community created of human freedom being exercised. Complete freedom since it means readiness to take up the cross (symbol of tortured death)!

The community is also a community of movement. The call does not say 'sit with me'. It says 'follow me'. It is a forward movement of self-denial. Isn't it rather strange that such a radical self-renunciation is expressed in terms of a forward movement? How can self-renunciation, the opposite of self-assertion, be a forward-directed movement? The secret is found in the 'me'. Who is the 'me'? He is the one heading towards death and resurrection, the ultimate self-renunciation and self-affirmation.

> ... who, though he was in the form of God, did not count equality with God a thing to be grasped, but emptied himself, taking the form of a servant, being born in the likeness of men. And being found in human form he humbled himself and became obedient unto death, even death on a cross. Therefore God has highly exalted him and bestowed on him the name which is above every name, that at the name of Jesus every knee should bow... Philippians 2:6-10

Thus, in following him we experience the paradox that self-renunciation is self-affirmation, self-affirmation is self-renunciation. This is the experience of salvation.

34

an
uncluttered meaningful
human relationship

I sat in a north Indian Hindu temple in Singapore.
Yes. I sat. There was no chair. On the concrete
floor was a carpet. On the carpet I sat down with a
Hindu friend. My mind soon began to sit down too.
Slowly but steadily my head became perceptive. I
noticed that the distance between my head and the
ceiling was greater than I was accustomed to. For
religious reflection a sitting posture is quite a con-
ducive arrangement for me. Later, I sat in a mosque
in Singapore. (There are seventy-seven mosques in
the Republic of Singapore.) Again, on the carpet, I
sat down. Here the distance between my head and
the ceiling was even greater than I had noticed in
the Hindu temple. I took time. I looked around
carefully. I watched the Muslims worshipping with
great reverence.

Neither place has chairs or benches. The place of
worship without chairs and benches carries a different atmosphere from the arrangement that we
know in the Christian churches. In the Hindu
temple and Islamic mosque the worshippers sit

35

down on the floor. Shoes removed!

The contrast between the Hindu temple and the mosque is tremendous. The Hindu temple is full of various mythological images while there is absolutely no image in the mosque. The mosque impresses me with its grand beauty of simplicity. Its simplicity and unclutteredness are charged with meaning. I remember that I experienced this sense of the beauty of Islam when I first visited the National Mosque in Kuala Lumpur years ago.

In Jakarta, a tremendous concrete National Mosque is approaching completion. It will be remembered by posterity as one of the most enduring gifts President Sukarno left to the people of Indonesia. One evening I walked in this Indonesian National Mosque. It is certainly one of the most impressive religious buildings I have ever seen, in its grandeur, in its beauty of line, and in its perfectly exquisite architectural proportions. I saw only a few people there. There will be many thousands coming here together when the building is completed. I sat down and looked up into the huge dome at the centre. I felt as though I were sitting at the very centre of the universe, the converging point of all meanings, the point which the philosopher calls the navel of the universe. Again I admired the simplicity and unclutteredness. The huge space is not an empty space. It is an uncluttered space. There is a definite difference between them.

All of a sudden I envied the people who will worship in this place. I would feel more at home worshipping the Father of Jesus Christ within this mosque-architecture than in the traditional church-architecture. I visualized Christian people, thousands of them, sitting on the floor of a church building built exactly like this Jakarta National Mosque (no chairs, no benches!) placing their Bibles on their laps and meditating on the Word of God who came for us, died for us, rose for us, and is coming for us. I remembered then that my Indonesian friend told me that the chief designer of this National Mosque is a Christian!

I was impressed as I walked through the inside of Saint Peter's in Rome. The inspiration one receives by being inside Saint Peter's is different from that experienced in the National Mosque in Kuala Lumpur and Jakarta. They speak a different language of emotion and inspiration. I admire both of them. I am proud of being a member of humanity whose spiritual energy is able to build such noble edifices.

Perhaps, personally, I am tired of *clutteredness*. When I drive, the Singapore streets are cluttered with 200,000 vehicles. The air I breathe is 'cluttered' with unbearable noises and fumes. In everything I do, I have to go through 'cluttered' systems. My human relationships are 'cluttered'. My economic life is 'cluttered'. There are simply so many things I bump into. I must be at all times at attention. When I walk into the church I bump into chairs! The whole world is cluttered. I miss uncluttered space. Yes! an uncluttered space but not an *empty* space. I don't want an empty space. Empty space means space without meaning. I want space which is uncluttered yet charged with meaning. Two classic arts of Japan, the tea ceremony and flower arranging, have given her people the sense of uncluttered space and uncluttered time charged with meaning.

I want to live in space which is charged with meaning—the kind of meaning that produces reconciliation and happiness in the community. Reconciliation and happiness do not come to us by cluttering our human space with all kinds of things. Then our human relationships would become just like a traffic jam in the street. No human inspiration can move around easily in such a 'traffic jam'. Reconciliation and happiness come from an uncluttered yet intensive inspiration. I am thinking of a beautiful story found in the Gospel where it is told that through one simple act of devotion cluttered space—human space—was rearranged, simplified and charged with tremendous redemptive meaning!

38

Now when Jesus was at Bethany in the house of Simon the leper, a woman came up to him with an alabaster jar of very expensive ointment, and she poured it on his head as he sat at table. But when the disciples saw it they were indignant, saying, 'Why this waste? For this ointment might have been sold for a large sum, and given to the poor.' But Jesus, aware of this, said to them, 'Why do you trouble the woman? For she has done a beautiful thing to me. For you always have the poor with you but you will not always have me. In pouring this ointment on my body she has done it to prepare me for burial. Truly, I say to you, wherever this gospel is preached in the whole world, what she has done will be told in memory of her'. Matthew 26:6-11

to be human

We are human. Quite evidently.

We have special qualities that distinguish us from all other animals. Zoologically we are the 'naked ape', but we have strange qualities that cannot be explained in the perspective of the 'naked ape'. We exercise freedom, and when we do this we are actually engaged in highly intellectual and psychological processes. We are able to observe happenings objectively and analyse the situation in great detail. There is an insurmountable gap between primate (ape) and human for the human mind is far superior to that of a chimpanzee. 'To be human' is a great privilege.

To us being human seems to be a very natural and automatic arrangement. 'I am a man so I am human'. That's it. Just as an orange is an orange, and an apple is an apple. It is, however, not that simple. 'I am a man and I am inhuman' is a genuine possibility and reality. What a terrible truth! Only a human can be inhuman. A chimpanzee can never become inhuman. (They may become 'in-ape'. I must ask the zoologist about this.) This destiny belongs only to humans.

Whether or not a man becomes human or inhuman is the most basic question posed to man. Human and inhuman, what an unpleasant contrast! How unsettling! But don't we usually behave like humans? We do some pretty bad things some times but even so inhuman situations do not occur too frequently. More often, perhaps, we find ourselves in between humanity and inhumanity—something like sub-human. 'To be a human' means, then, freedom from 'sub-human' and 'inhuman'. Any tendency towards the direction of 'sub-human' and 'inhuman' threatens 'to be human'. Isn't this self-evident?

Not quite. We must ask ourselves, what does 'to be human' mean? 'To be human' means to live in relationship. An isolated individualistic life is hardly human life. True, man is man whether he moves in community or lives in isolation. But the 'isolated man' is far less lively and with less personality than the 'engaged man' (the Samaritan in the parable of Jesus). When man meets man—a great human event!—he is engaged and then his personality comes out most powerfully. Then he becomes actively human.

'To live in *human* relationship with other men', is the substance of 'to be human'. Oppression, exploitation, persecution, discrimination—all these are not human relationships but the experience of sub-human and inhuman relationships. Human re-

41

lationship then, means the relationship of 'love your neighbour as yourself'. (Leviticus 19:18)

> The commandments, 'You shall not commit adultery, you shall not kill, you shall not steal, you shall not covet', and any other commandment, are summed up in this sentence, 'You shall love your neighbour as yourself'. Romans 13:9

> For the whole law is fulfilled in one word, 'You shall love your neighbour as yourself'. Galatians 5:14

How difficult it is!

> Therefore because you trample upon the poor
> and take from him exactions of wheat,
> you have built houses of hewn stone,
> but you have not dwelt in them;
> you have planted pleasant vineyards,
> but you shall not drink their wine. Amos 5:11

to define man?

Suppose my son says: 'My father is forty-two years old. He was born in Japan. He has Japanese short legs and long torso. (*Most Japanese tend to have more body and facial hair than other mongoloid groups, and skin colour is more often brown than yellowish. Body build tends to be sturdy. Encyclopaedia Britannica.*) He is kind and generous at times but the reverse at others. He likes raw fish and *sukiyaki*. He teaches theology—his field is, whatever it means, systematic theology. He has many books.'

These are true facts. They show who I am and what I am. But I do not think these observations, however detailed they may be, can be taken as a definition of me. Kosuke Koyama. They describe me, that is all. They cannot grasp me. They cannot as it were, nail me down. I am still free! And secretly I enjoy, as I am sure you do too, being indefinable. The English verb 'define' comes from the Latin word *definire* (*de*—from, *finire*—to set a limit to, from *finis*—a boundary). I cannot fly. Flying is beyond my boundary. I cannot be an angel. An angelic life is beyond my boundary. These are rather obvious boundaries and do not bother me. 'Kosuke Koyama cannot fly' is very limited information about me anyway. But as we carefully examine all kinds of valid and meaningful boundaries for man we become aware that there is some strange quality in man which cannot be defined. We speak of the emergence of 'technological man'. It seems to me the word 'man' indicates some quality which refuses to be completely controlled by any word that comes before it, whether 'religious man', 'capitalist man' or 'organization man'. He goes beyond the boundaries!

This is how a monkey is defined:

> MONKEY is a common name for many mammals of the order *Primates*. Strictly speaking, monkeys include only the group with long tails and short, narrow faces. This leaves out the apes and lemurs. Apes are larger than monkeys and have either no tails or very short ones. But some monkeys, including baboons, also have no tails. The apes include gorillas, chimpanzees, orangutans, and gibbons.
>
> The name *monkey* probably comes from an Italian word meaning *old woman*. It may refer to the monkey's face, which looks like that of a wrinkled old woman.
>
> (The World Book Encyclopaedia.)

We can accept this as being accurate. But as soon as we come across a definition of man, we want to challenge it.

> MAN is the most remarkable of all the creatures that lives in all climates, makes and uses tools, creates fire, prays, talks and destroys his own kind in wars. Through science, man has unlocked many secrets of the universe, such as knowledge of the shape of the earth, the structure of atoms, and the composition of plants and animals.
>
> (The World Book Encyclopaedia.)

44

We question whether this is right or not since we are the ones who are defining man. No chicken has attempted to define chicken (or man). The ability to stand off and look at himself critically is the unique characteristic of man. And when he looks at himself man becomes 'his own most vexing problem' (R. Niebuhr). Quite obviously man is too 'wild' to be contained in a definition. We can describe him but we cannot go any further. Any description, however full, gives us only an *outline* of 'what is man'. His inner quality, *freedom*, which makes up the centre of his personality, refuses to be nailed down. Freedom is rooted deeply in man's quality of being man. It is a quality which refuses to be controlled externally, Dr V. E. Frankl, who survived Nazi death concentration camp, speaks of his own experience:

> We who lived in concentration camps can remember the men who walked through the huts comforting others, giving away their last piece of bread. They may have been few in number, but they offer sufficient proof that everything can be taken from a man but one thing: the last of human freedoms—to choose one's attitude in any given set of circumstances, to choose one's own way.
>
> And there were always choices to make. Every day, every hour, offered the opportunity to make a decision, a decision which determined whether you would or would not submit to those powers which threatened to rob you of your very self, your inner freedom; which determined whether or not you would become the plaything of circumstances, renouncing freedom and dignity to become moulded into the form of the typical inmate.
>
> (Man's Search for Meaning. p.104)

When I write like this, I do not mean that man's freedom is something we can fully understand. It seems to me that man's freedom is a mystery to

45

himself. I am 'free' to decide between bread and rice for my breakfast. Freedom, I am thinking now, is something of more serious character than this. May I say it is 'freedom to love one's neighbour'? Only when one loves someone, is one ready to be 'nailed down'. There love, as it were, locates and clarifies freedom. When love works, the character of freedom reveals itself—even though it is still a mystery to us. 'Greater love has no man than this, that a man lay down his life for his friends.' (John 15:13) Man has the freedom to love and 'lay down his life for his friends'. When he chooses to become 'unfree' for the sake of others, he is most free and most loving. There he is 'nailed down'. This is the story of the mystery of 'definition of man'.

> For I decided to know nothing among you except Jesus Christ and him crucified. I Corinthians 2:2

cruel nonsense

A student from Sarawak at Trinity College passed away in the General Hospital from a kidney ailment about a year ago. He was a young man with a great promise of life. He was taken away from our world suddenly and cruelly. He was snatched away from the ones who loved him. He was *very much* taken away from the ones who loved him *very much*. If you had loved him as much as you love your own life (his mother did!) when he was taken away, your life would have been taken away. You would be lifeless. You would be dead too.

The intensity of tragedy is proportionate to the intensity of love. 'If you don't want to suffer, do not love.' Isn't this the ultimate advice that the Enlightened Buddha gave to mankind? Isn't this profoundly true? Who suffered most at the death of this young man? His mother. No one suffered more than she did. It is because no one loved him more than she did. He came from her. She nourished him from the beginning of his life. He was her own extention. She suffered intensely because she was involved with him intensely.

47

For her the death of her son was totally and absolutely unacceptable. Anything else may have been acceptable. But not this. She refused to accept the fact that her son was dead. No amount of preaching, no amount of Christian theology, no pension or gift could help her. She was confronted by the real power of death that separated her from her son. Death is an ultimate separation, the ultimate breakdown of communication and sharing. This is what she experienced between herself and her son. Death is the enemy of love.

You may say that death is not ultimate. Death is only a passageway to the better world. But I take death very seriously. If I die, my body will rot, or if I am cremated it will become ashes. It seems to me that there is an ultimate difference between the living Koyama and Koyama who has become ashes. Jesus took his death very seriously. 'Father, if thou art willing remove this cup (death on the cross) from me; nevertheless not my will, but thine be done. And there appeared to him an angel from heaven, strengthening him. And being in an agony he prayed more earnestly; and his sweat became like great drops of blood falling down upon the ground' (Luke 22:42-44). Christianity becomes superficial and illusory when Christians speak about death carelessly and lightly. If death is not a matter of ultimate importance then 'while we were yet sinners Christ died for us' (Romans 5:8) does not change anything ultimately either.

At the funeral service, I was a spectator since it was not the funeral of my son. I was protected by a safe distance from the tragedy. That afternoon, all of us were spectators. There was a decisive line drawn between the mother and the rest of us. For the spectators it was important that a Christian funeral service proceed *properly*. There should be prayers, preaching and singing. These make up a worship service. A service is a formal (dressed-up) function. It was a time for Christians to show their belief in the power of Jesus Christ who defeated the power of death.

But dressed-up spectators cannot make witness to the power of Christ that defeated the power of death. In the villages of India, family-planning officers urge men to accept vasectomy as they themselves have done. They are not spectators and this witness works. There was one person who disturbed the whole funeral service. That person was a non-spectator, the victim, the mother herself. For the spectators the service was 'meaningful', 'Christian' and 'necessary'. But for her it was obviously nonsense. No, it was more than nonsense. It was cruel nonsense. She was not listening to what was said. She was not participating in the service. She wanted to be near her son. She wanted to speak to him, to embrace him. She loved him.

The spectators could not tolerate such an unruly outburst. Expression of such intense motherly love was embarrassing during this *proper* divine service. So someone physically held the agonized mother in her seat. Her son was right there. But she was prevented from approaching him. How cruel! I wonder if there was any theological, psychological, medical or pastoral justification for that. Perhaps there was. But why didn't we prepare a different situation so that she could be with her son privately? Was the funeral service more important than the expression of the mother's love? Why did the spectators make a spectacle out of her? Death is inhuman. Man is mortal so to die is human. It is true none of us lives for ever but strangely to die is also inhuman. When our loved ones die we want a funeral service. I understand this. But it must be a comfort to the bereaved. 'The sabbath (funeral service) was made for man, not man for the sabbath (funeral service)' (Mark 2:27).

Every cry of the mother's disturbed the service. The spectators thought that a Christian should be more controlled. Doesn't a Christian have hope? There was even a whisper to the effect that she cried because she was not a Christian. The spectators had cool heads. The victim had a hot heart. Dear friends, I am a Christian. I would cry more than that woman did if I were in a similar situation. I tell you this quite frankly and seriously. I am human. I am not a devil. I am not an angel. I am not super-human. I am not a monster. I am not God. I am human. God created me so. I thank God for this. If a loved one was taken from me I would cry. If I am human I react as a human. If I am not human how can I be a Christian? Isn't this point quite clear as we study the stories of Abraham, Isaac, Jacob, Moses, Job, Hosea, Jeremiah, Isaiah and so on in the Old Testament and also the New Testament apostles. Didn't Jesus cry out on the cross when God whom he loved and who loved him hid himself from Jesus: 'My God, my God, why hast thou forsaken me?' (Mark 13:34)

We Christians do inhuman things from time to time. We condemn the deep cry that comes out of the human soul. We place more importance on how this or that looks to both Christians and outsiders. For us how we appear to others is quite important. God heard the mother's cry. It was a cry of love. It was sincere. He understood it.

neighbour-logical theology

Theology is a gift from God. It is so because it is God who initiates 'God-talk' to man. Theology is man's response to the God who speaks to man and comes to man. God is not a silent God. God is a speaking God. He intends to establish the reality of *communion* with man in this concrete world of ours. When we say 'theology' we mean this special kind of theology which was initiated by God who comes to us. This peculiar character of theology is not self-evident. It is a hidden reality. That God is speaking to us today and that He is ruling the histories of nations and the communities is not obvious and self-evident to everyone. Theology is a 'not-self-evident' science. Theology and faith go together. Faith is a total personal commitment. Christian theology is a 'committed thinking' involving spirit, soul and mind.

The way God has spoken and is speaking is 'historical'. He spoke to man through the historical experiences of the people of Israel, the Church, and the nations, great and small. His historical talk was responsible talk. Theology is responsible talk. It is responsible talk to one's neighbours. Theology is talk that takes one's neighbours seriously. 'Love your neighbour as yourself' (Luke 10:27). Theology is deeply 'neighbour-logical'. Jesus Christ is a 'neighbour-logical' man. 'His name shall be called Emmanuel (which means, God with us)' (Matthew 1:23).

'Theology in Action' is a 'neighbour-logical' concept. It means 'to engage in theology together with one's neighbours'. It is a humble attempt. It hopes to contribute to the ministry of the Church. There are all kinds of neighbours: rich, poor, strong, weak, educated, uneducated, oppressing and oppressed, ... whoever they are, 'neighbour-logical' theology must take them seriously. In saying this, we are not making ourselves super-humans who are able to involve ourselves with everybody. We who engage in 'neighbour-logical' theology acknowledge, with humility, our spiritual and mental limitations. The reality of one's neighbours—all that they are and all that they do—must become a motivating force for our theological engagement.

We find ourselves in various concrete situations. Various situations demand various formulations of theology. In certain life-situations the theology of incarnation may speak vividly of God's presence, but in other situations it may be the theology of creation or redemption or resurrection or the Church. Amazingly theology is not 'rigid', it is 'dynamic'. It finds its integrity in pointing to Jesus Christ the Head of the Church and the Head of the cosmos (Colossians 1:15-20).

anthropology by god

Ichthyology (what a big word!) is fish-understanding. (*Ichthy*—fish, *logy*—understanding). It speaks about fish. Theology (another big word!) is God-understanding (*theo*—God, *logy*—understanding). It speaks about God. Fish understanding, I would think, is more direct than God-understanding.

The reason is obvious. Fish we can catch: from guppies to sharks, from piranhas to trout. We can catch them and study their behaviour, dissect them and see their organs. We can take our time and consult other authorities when necessary. We have control over the fish, the object of our studies. God-understanding is quite different. We cannot catch Him, watch Him or open Him up. 'God is Spirit' (John 4:24). In fish-understanding man observes and studies fish. In God-understanding man is, as it were, studied by God. It is—let me be a little confusing here—an anthropology (man-understanding) by God, a very special kind of anthropology.

Anthropology is, of course, man's understanding of himself. It is really a tremendous undertaking. Any textbook on anthropology makes evident its immense scope: pre-historic man, man studied through heredity, genetics, race, evolution, culture, tools, food gathering, clothing, shelter, transport, economics, family-life, management, political organization, religion, language, art, education, and other aspects. When I say theology is anthropology by God I do not mean that we have a comprehensive textbook on anthropology written by God. Theology as 'man-understanding by God' means that theology is man's understanding of God on the basis of God's understanding of man. It is as a child understands his mother only by way of his mother's far more intense and profound understanding of the child. Theology does not and cannot just speak about God apart from man. Theology is then, 'God-man-ology'.

stories within me

I am a forty-two-year-old Japanese man. I have lived with millions of other Japanese through a time of unprecedented transition, or should I say, a time of radical discontinuity of national life. It was within this very short span of forty-two years or so that old Japan was brought to judgement and the new Japan came into being. I belong to both the old Japan and the new Japan. I lived my first sixteen years under (the Meiji) Imperial Constitution promulgated in 1889. The following twenty-six years I have lived under the postwar New Constitution of Japan (1946). My life has, as you can see, been 'constitutionally' divided into sixteen and twenty-six. The supreme authority of the Japanese state was located in the sacred inviolable personage of the Emperor under the old Constitution. The system was authoritarian. The New Constitution expresses the best democratic principles for the welfare of man and state. It is democratic. I find myself an 'authoritarian self' and a 'democratic self'.

'Authoritarian self' and 'democratic self' in one person? Yes. It is, I assure you, quite a troublesome arrangement. It pushes me into a turmoil of self-identity, and it also confuses others who try to judge my thoughts and actions. Sometimes I envy those who live under one arrangement. Salt-water fish live in salt water. Fresh-water fish live in fresh water. That is a healthy arrangement. But suppose a salt-water fish were put into fresh water. This would certainly produce a 'constitutional' difficulty. This is, more or less, what has happened to me. When I say I see an 'authoritarian I' and a 'democratic I' within myself, I mean that I find within myself two histories: the authoritarian history of Japan up to the end of the war, and her democratic post-war history. This statement is a bold simplification, but it expresses the kind of tension I experience within myself today.

Having two selves means two kinds of experience, and two kinds of history within myself. The concepts of 'person' and 'history' are inseparable. Both are mysteries when we try to grasp them. But we can at least say that each one of us lives the life of a 'person' in 'history'. We cannot think of a person except in 'history', nor can we speak of 'history' if persons are not present. Let me illustrate this: the old history taught Japanese boys that the kitchen is a woman's domain and it is not fitting for men or boys to enter or meddle in kitchen affairs. Whatever is prepared men should eat 'without comment'. Consequently no Japanese man washes dishes! The new history is teaching Japanese boys that the kitchen is for every member of the family.

It is a place of family democracy. Consequently today you can see a Japanese man washing dishes with his wife, or even such an 'outrageous' situation as his wife reading the newspaper while he washes up! This shows how the character of history determines the pattern of family life and the personality of the individual person.

human-value

What is human value? One prominent Singaporean answered this question at a recent study gathering: 'You and I know what human value is. I think what the Ten Commandments are trying to say—that is human value.' His point, in short, is this: 'to honour your father and your mother'—this is human value; 'not to kill'—this is human value; 'not to commit adultery'—this is human value; 'not to steal'—this is human value; 'not to bear false witness'—this is human value. I think this is an answer with insight, and I must say that I agree with him.

Something valuable is something good, something creative, something that contributes to man's life in his community. Something without value is something bad, something destructive, something that makes man despair, something that damages his life in his community.

Certainly, we do have some idea about human value. In fact, to be human means to know human value. In the Bible, human value is discussed, evaluated and appreciated in a certain special context. What is this special context? It is the context of the *preamble* –Exodus 20:2. 'I am the Lord, your God, who brought you out of the land of Egypt, out of the house of bondage.' The Ten Commandments will be like a sailing boat floating on the windless ocean if they are to be understood apart from the preamble. What the Ten Commandments are saying is this: 'You see, I have saved you. And you are saved. I am God who is interested in salvation. I, the saving God, am giving you these Commandments.'

At this point, may I venture some generalizations; I think two views could emerge. Mr A might say something like this: 'Well, so what! What difference does this preamble of an old religion make? Remember we are living today in the twentieth century. We are not walking in the Sinai desert. With or without preamble, "not to kill!" that's all. Theologians make simple things complicated. We had better keep God out of the picture. As soon as He comes in everything gets mixed up!'

Mr B might feel quite differently: 'How helpful it is to know that all human values are placed in God's context of salvation. I did not know this interesting relationship between human value and—pardon my using an awkward expression—God-value. (God is interested in man's salvation. Salvation of man then must be of value to God. Isn't that so?) To me, this relationship between human value and God-value opens up a new horizon of understanding in my mind. Particularly it helps me to interpret hu-

man value. I think I know what human value is,
but I have been having difficulty determining what
that value is in my life and how to interpret it.'

There are millions of Mr A's and Mr B's in this
world. That 'human value is rooted in God-value'
is a fundamental principle of Christian theology
and ethics.

'Do not steal' is a human value. I agree. But isn't
it a fact that I do steal? Perhaps not in the way that
a thief robs a bank, but in a subtle way? Isn't it true
that often stealing takes place on a gigantic scale,
between classes in a community or even between
nations? We know what human values are, but they
cannot be easily realized in our world. At this
point of difficulty, we are forced to interpret human value in a more involved way. There are many
interpretations possible of the relationship between
human value and its realization in our world.
Mr B's argument on human value is guided by the
God-value which is expressed in Apostle Paul's
words:

> While we were yet helpless, at the right time Christ died for
> the ungodly. Why, one will hardly die for a righteous man—
> though perhaps for a good man one will dare even to die.
> But God shows his love for us in that while we were yet sin-
> ners Christ died for us. Romans 5:6-8

God values us so highly His Son gave His life.
This 'proof of his love towards us' drives us to feel
the depth of the Mind of God who says, 'You shall
not steal'. We not only know 'you shall not steal'
but we also know the Mind of the One who commands this human value. Thus our knowledge of

'you shall not steal' becomes *personal* knowledge. It is the commandment that has come not from a stranger but from the One whom we know.

Human value is illuminated by God-value. Human value is nourished and healthy, as long as we see the Mind of God behind it. Our knowledge of God-value leads up to a richer and deeper understanding of human value. This special knowledge is not magical power that can enable us to materialize human value with ease. But certainly it will give us courage and wisdom as we live in today's world in which human value is often distorted.

education seen by theology

Paul says that Christ is the Head, the Beginning, and the Firstborn of all creation. He is the Head of the total creation! 'In him all things were created'. The same Christ is the head of the Church, the redeemed community. He is the Head, the Beginning and the Firstborn 'from the dead'. He is in everything pre-eminent. There are not two heads, one for the creation and one for the Church. (Colossians 1:15-20)

Through this Head and for this Head all things 'in heaven and on earth' are to be reconciled. Reconciliation is the work of God through this all pre-eminent Christ. It took this *fullness* of Christ to accomplish reconciliation. The New Testament reconciliation is abundant reconciliation ('grace upon grace'—John 1:16).

Education is ultimately concerned with man's relationship with the *whole* which is created 'in him'. Since this whole is now a *reconciled whole* in God in Christ (II Corinthians 5:19) man must be brought to realize the depth of this new *educational* arrangement. And is not this the grand theme and subject of education?

Thus, when we speak of reconciliation, we are speaking of salvation in which we find the goal of education. In this reconciliation, theology and education meet.

> So if you are offering your gift at the altar and there remember that your brother has something against you; leave your gift there before the altar and go, first be reconciled to your brother, and then come and offer your gift.
> Matthew 5:23-24

I see in this straightforward warning of the Lord an encounter between theology and education which is full of implications. How embarrassing and inconvenient it is to remember at the most sacred moment of divine worship that 'your brother has something against you'. The Lord says that you must delay your act of offering a gift. But you must not delay the act of reconciliation. Go! and be reconciled! Why cannot reconciliation be delayed? It is the work of the Head of the universe and the Church. This is the mind of Christ the Reconciler, through whom the new age of worship has come.

Then does not Matthew 5:23-24 speak of the central concern of education theologically grounded? How can we find the genuine value of education apart from man's finding his place in the created and reconciled world? And how can education become real—as real as the Word which became flesh (John 1:14)—unless we go through the educational process of 'leaving our gift' and have the new experience of 'first being reconciled'! What a great theological educational value is discovered when we remember that our brother has something against us *there* in front of the altar!

The reconciliation is wrought in the freedom of God. God, in his freedom, acted 'in him' to reconcile the universe to Himself. The spirit of slavery, then, must not step into our education (Galatians 4:7). We remember, in our freedom, that our brother has something against us, and, in our freedom, leave our gift and go! When this happens education becomes a *present* and *concrete* life experience. What else is more *present* and more *concrete* than the experience of reconciliation? Is there anything more *educational* than the experience of reconciliation?

Sometime in the early sixties, while he was in prison, Paul wrote the message of the abundant reconciliation. 'Remember my fetters!' (Colossians 4:18 cf. 3:10) He was an 'educated man' since he was able to place himself in the total saving history of God and speak of the freedom of Christian man even though he was in fetters. It seems to me that the value and character of education should be judged according to the degree to which it can bring man, in spite of all kinds of 'fetters' (you can name them!) to the experience of freedom in the context of God's act of reconciliation.

two hands versus one thousand hands

The Buddha's image always invites me to reflect upon something deeper than the concerns of everyday life. How much is this month's petrol bill for my car? Which 'plane should I take to Hong Kong? Should I close the windows in case it rains while I am out? All these are everyday concerns. We do have a lot of them. As a matter of fact, most of the time we live from one everyday concern to another.

The image of the Buddha comes to me always as a reminder of the importance of meditation. He sits stately, with no hint of unbalance or precariousness. His eyes are open, benevolent, attentive and intelligent. His ears and mouth are ever ready for the communication of the Four Noble Truths which involve a discussion much deeper than do the concerns of everyday. Standing in front of the image I hear his last words: 'Decay is inherent in all compound things. Work out your own salvation with diligence'. This is a simple and yet strong message. I wonder what these last words mean. Has anyone other than the one who said them ever really understood them?

In the New Delhi National Museum the Buddha's image came to me almost as salvation after my head was utterly confused by the strange and complicated Hindu images, particularly by those that have more than two hands. I experienced the same sensation in the Tokyo National Museum where I saw many Japanese Buddhist images that have more than two hands. I missed Thai Buddhism, which has no images of 'many hands'. Many-handed images, for some psychological reason, bother me. Many-handed images are common in the Hindu tradition. Vishnu as the creator Narayana has four hands. Vishnu traversing the universe seems to have six hands. Vishnu and Lakshmi on the Serpent Ananta, afloat on the primeval waters, have four hands. The evil Ravana has twenty arms.

In Japanese Buddhism there are four kinds of Buddha (*Sakay*—a historical Gotama; *Yakushi*—a Medicine-Man-Buddha; *Amida*—the Merciful Divine Saviour, and *Dai-ni-chi*—the philosophically conceived Buddha) and therefore four kinds of image of the Buddha. But they are so much alike and the way to distinguish between them is by studying the forms their fingers make. They have only two hands as we do. But when we come to the Japanese *Kwan-non* group of images we encounter those with many hands. The devotion to 'the *Kwan-non* of a thousand hands' was introduced towards the middle of the eighth century from China by the Japanese monk Genbo. At that time images were actually made with a thousand hands; eighteen or forty hands were of relatively large size and the other (982 or 960) hands were made to look like rays emanating from the back of the image. On the hands which hold nothing an eye is painted to complete a *Kwan-non* of 'A thousand hands a thousand eyes'. After the ninth century, however, the general trend was to give the so-called thousand-hand *Kwan-non* only forty symbolic hands. They are made to appear serene and *infinitely merciful*.

The thousand hands and thousand eyes are not an expression of grotesque monstrosity. They symbolize the preparedness of the *Kwan-non* to come to the help of man. 'Kwan' means 'to see', 'Non' means 'sound'. Literally the Japanese word *Kwan-non* means the 'one who sees the sound'. Here is a profound 'confusion'. We understand what it is to *hear* sound. What is meant, of course, is that the *Kwan-non* hears the cry of man who needs salvation, but his *hearing includes seeing* as when a mother sees intuitively and instantly her child upon hearing his cry. The *Kwan-non* image reminds me of the famous Exodus passage:

> Then the Lord said, 'I have seen the affliction of my people who are in Egypt, and have heard their cry because of their taskmasters; I know their sufferings, and I have come down to deliver them out of the hand of the Egyptians, ...' Exodus 3:7

I personally fail to appreciate the Hindu symbolism of many hands. It is abrasive to my sensitivities. With the Japanese *Kwan-non* images of many hands (not all *Kwan-nons* have many hands) I feel less difficulty, perhaps because they are made in a Japanese way and their facial expressions are familiar to me. Even so I do feel mental hesitation. The symbolism of many hands did not originate in Japan. It is traced back to the ancient Hindu mythology.

Many-hands symbolism is too strong for me (it is like Indian curry). I like to have a more subtle or veiled symbolism. Physiologically, 'many hands' (and 'many eyes') appear as a monstrous deformity. To try to communicate the message of the 'preparedness to meet the needs of man' through such an intensive deformity is certainly a striking enterprise of man's imagination. I can understand its intention and meaning. Yet I feel psychological difficulty with it. My mind is perhaps not imaginative enough.

I love two normal hands. No matter how busy and how limited they may be, I love the normal two hands. I have two hands. I saw my mother work with her two hands for these many years running her big busy family. Her two hands are ever prepared to help her children's needs. I see a pianist

69

making most inspiring music with two hands, and a surgeon transplanting a kidney with his two hands. When Jesus was crucified his two hands were nailed down. My human experience is so deeply rooted in the reality of the two hands that the suggestion (symbolism) of one person having more than two hands, *thereby* indicating preparedness in mercy and love, almost seems to me to be going against the very meaning that 'many hands' and 'many eyes' are trying to communicate.

In short, I feel two normal hands and two normal eyes will do a much better job in communication of mercy and love. Two hands may be far more limited than a thousand hands in their activities, but the *limitation* of two hands can convey in its own profound way how deeply and extensively prepared they are to help and save others. That which is limited has more explosive, more spiritual (and religious) power than that which is not limited. We are living today in a world which gives immediate approval and commendation to the human striving after 'the limitless' (limitless power, limitless prestige, limitless prosperity ...) rather than 'the limited'. Perhaps we must read carefully an observation Jesus made as he watched what a poor widow did:

> He looked up and saw the rich putting their gifts into the treasury, and he saw a poor widow put in two copper coins. And he said, 'Truly I tell you, this poor widow has put in more than all of them; for they all contributed out of their abundance, but she out of her poverty put in all the living that she had'. Luke 21:1-4

The Apostle Paul speaks of the power of the grace of God working through his *limited* life:

> And to keep me from being too elated by the abundance of revelations, a thorn was given me in the flesh, a messenger of Satan, to harass me, to keep me from being too elated. Three times I besought the Lord about this, that it should leave me; but he said to me, 'My grace is sufficient for you, for my power is made perfect in weakness'. II Corinthians 12:7-9

Paul goes on to speak in the same manner of Jesus Christ:

> For he was crucified in weakness, but lives by the power of God. II Corinthians 13:4

do as a buddhist does

Thailand owes very much to Buddhist monks. From the beginning of its nationhood, Buddhist monks have been active in works of mercy, hospitals and schools. Even today in the rural areas of the kingdom schools are located in Buddhist temples. The monks have taught moral precepts. Over the centuries they have provided the first inspirations to a host of creative minds in the production of literature, music, painting and sculpture. They are a blessing to Thailand. And they are a blessing to the world. Christians must be the first to acknowledge and thank God for all the good the monks have done for the people of Thailand. It is dangerous to think that only Christians can perform acts of mercy. This monopoly-psychology is arrogant both in the sight of man and of God.

Often I am reminded that Jesus Christ was present among the peoples of the world even before the arrival of missionaries, Christians and churches. He goes ahead of us. He does not follow us. He says, 'follow me!' (Matthew 4:19). While Paul was on the way to Damascus, he was already there. 'Who are you, Lord', he said, and the voice answered, 'I am Jesus, whom you are persecuting...' (Acts 9:5). Paul stands in line with Jeremiah:

> Before I formed you in the womb I knew you, and before you were born I consecrated you; I appointed you a prophet to the nations. Jeremiah 1:5

The hidden presence of Jesus—'In the beginning was the word'! (John 1:1)—among the Buddhist expresses itself in unexpected ways. On numerous occasions I have observed that Buddhists practise what Jesus commands. Without knowing his name they give the hungry food, the thirsty drink, take a stranger home, clothe the naked, nurse the sick and visit prisoners (Matthew 25:33-36). They may be quite surprised in the end to know that '... as you did it to one of the least of these my brethren, you did it to me' (v.40)! Perhaps they do what they do in the name of Buddha. Is feeding the hungry, clothing the naked, visiting prisoners in the name of the Buddha an act of no value in the light of the name of Jesus Christ? Impossible!

> There will be tribulation and distress for every human being who does evil, the Jew first and also the Greek, but glory and honour and peace for every one who does good, the Jew first and also the Greek. For God shows no partiality. Romans 2:9-11

Too often a man who does not confess the name of Jesus Christ practises the love of God, and a man who calls himself a Christian fails to show concern. 'Not every one who says to me, "Lord, Lord," shall enter the kingdom of heaven, but he who does the will of my Father who is in heaven' (Matthew 7:21). I understand this parable to be a sharp *warning* to the pride of the Christian Church. Knowing his name must mean 'practising his name'. This calls for special judgement. 'For the time has come for judgement to begin with the household of God...' (I Peter 4:17)

When we understand what 'Samaritans' meant to the Jews of Jesus' time, we are amazed at his boldness in making the Samaritan of the parable the one who became a neighbour to the attacked one. There was such a terrible Jewish antipathy against the Samaritans that one questioned by Jesus even avoided the unpleasantness of mentioning the word 'Samaritan' and answered instead '... The one who showed mercy on him' (Luke 10:37).

This parable then must have been a terrible affront to the Jews. It confronts us directly today in Asia when we see the 'Samaritan' as a Hindu or a Buddhist. And Jesus says to us 'Go and do likewise'! This is a humbling thought. We can be thankful that our God is a universal God. We are at the same time humbled by a sharp admonition when Buddhists do as Jesus commanded. This makes our Christian life possible since there is no Christian life apart from humility (Philippians 2:1-11).

'ear-lids'

In the course of a few months Hong Kong's skyline has changed. New ultra-modern buildings are shooting up. Jakarta is beginning to have hotels of international standing. Singapore is an island fast becoming a concrete jungle. Foundation concrete blocks are being pounded down by steam hammers with tremendous power and nerve-racking din. And here in this small island (Singapore) we are learning to live with the roar and clangour of construction sites. There is no escape, and by the time every empty space has been built on, these buildings will be demolished and the construction of even-more-up-to-date buildings will take place. It has been pointed out by some experts that the buildings being constructed in Singapore today are too solid and too strong. Builders should take into account the cost of demolition since buildings are bound to become obsolete in this rapidly changing technological society. Urban renewal programmes will continue for many decades to come. From now on men on this planet will be non-stop builders. So we might as well learn to live amid construction sites and their incessant din. We are in for an era of 'super-din'.

When I think about our ears (let me remind you I am not a biologist) I have a hunch that our bodies are not ready for the 'super-din' era. Our ears are obviously not equipped to deal with the tidal wave of noise. Our minds may understand, but I am sure our ears (hearing nerve system) are not ready for it.

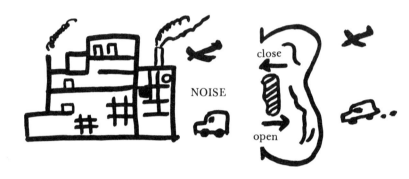

Our eyes have lids and pupils to protect them from excessive light, but unfortunately we do not have ear-lids to shut out unbearable noise. How convenient it would be to have ear-lids which could give us instant quiet in this world of din. It may take millions of years for us to develop ear-lids! Meanwhile, what can we do? One solution might be to move to a remote mountain district, but then how will we make a living? Alternatively we could build a sound-proof house—but how expensive that would be! I wonder just how much our minds have suffered over the last twenty years or so as we move into the super-noise era. Have we learned to live with noise, and the fact that we cannot progress without it? How many have died prematurely because of super-noise? How much has it hampered good intellectual thinking? Technology took such a sudden giant stride that it has confused the pace of biological evolution. Our ears are unprepared, but super-din is already here. This gap may be bridged in time by the invention of soundless equipment and machines (another technological stride!) but *meanwhile* how can we survive without damaging our precious human minds? How shall we survive the time between 'noise-creating technology' and 'noise-eradicating technology'? We await eagerly the coming of the latter. Only when the former and the latter come to us as one unit can the technological world enjoy relative happiness.

Our minds have an amazing facility for adjusting to all kinds of situations so we may well survive—but I fear not as 'fully human' beings. Too great an adjustment may be performed at the expense of man's human life quality.

missionary controversy

'In the beginning was the Word and the Word was with God, and the Word was God' (John 1:1). Man owes his very existence to the Word of God. '... he might make you know that man does not live by bread alone, but that man lives by everything that proceeds out of the mouth of the Lord' (Deuteronomy 8:3). In the perspective of the Christian faith 'all things hold together in Christ' (Colossians 1:17). The Incarnate Word of God (John 1:14) holds 'all things' in his incarnation, crucifixion, resurrection and ascension. He is today, right in this turbulent chapter of mankind, the Head of the Church and the world (Colossians 1:18-20). God who spoke the Primary Word at the beginning is speaking today and will speak to us in the future (Hebrews 13:8). God who expresses himself at the beginning will express himself at the end. His Primary Word is his End Word and his End Word is His Primary Word. 'I am the Alpha and the Omega, the beginning and the end' (Revelation 21:6).

'In the beginning was the Word and the Word was with God, and the Word was God.' This is *the* basis for all theological education. *If* at the beginning God did *not* express himself, if someone other than God himself spoke the primary word, if God remained silent about man and history, that is to say, if in the beginning there was absolute silence—then, how can 'theology' in the genuine Christian sense be possible? How can we study the Word of God if he is 'wordless', silent? How can we read a letter when we do not find one in our letter box? (We may be able to forge one, but a forged letter, no matter how well it is written, is never a genuine letter!)

The Word that 'proceedeth out of the mouth of God' is the mighty and responsible word. 'So shall my word be that goes forth from my mouth; it shall not return to me empty, but it shall accomplish that which I purpose, and prosper in the thing for which I sent it' (Isaiah 55:11). The Word which shall 'accomplish that which I purpose' is the Word of Covenant between God and man, the Word spoken in God's faithful and committed relationship with man. The Word of Covenant is the Word of involvement. The Word of Involvement is not an easy-going loose-end. The Word attacks, destroys, builds, comforts, saves man. The Word of God is dynamic! It is indeed the Word that arouses controversy! 'Hear the word of the Lord, O People of Israel; for the Lord has a *controversy* with the inhabitants of the land. There is no faithfulness or kindness, and no knowledge of God in the land...' (Hosea 4:1). 'Controversy' here means 'strife', 'a

79

noisy quarrel'. The cognate Arabic means 'agitation' and 'disquietude'. It is one of the crucial words which expresses God's 'agitated mind' for the salvation of his people and the world. If God discarded his Covenant then he would be free from this 'agitation'. Why doesn't he forget about man and the Covenant? He is faithful at the beginning and at the end! So God has become the God of controversy. The controversy initiated by the Covenant God is called the Primary Controversy. From this Primary Controversy emerges 'missionary controversy'. 'And he entered the synagogue and for three months spoke boldly, arguing and pleading about the kingdom of God...' (Acts 19:8). It would be a fake and misleading 'missionary controversy' if it were not rooted in the Primary Controversy. On the other hand missionary controversy (missionary here, of course, means all Christians) will be lively and meaningful when it *dares*, with prayer and hard work, to present the message (Jesus Christ) of the Primary Controversy in the most 'striking' and 'meaningful' way to men today.

commercial battle

I understand that the heart of the doctrine of the Buddha is found in the Four Noble Truths:

1. What now, O monks, is the noble truth of Suffering? Birth is suffering, old age is suffering, death is suffering, sorrow, lamentations, pain, grief and despair are suffering.

2. But what, O monks, is the noble truth of the Origin of suffering? It is that Craving, which gives rise to fresh re-birth and, bound up with pleasure and lust, now here now there, finds ever fresh delight.

3. But what, O monks, is the noble truth of the Extinction of suffering? It is the complete fading away and extinction of this Craving, its forsaking and giving up, liberation and detachment from it.

4. But what, O monks, is the noble truth of the path leading to the extinction of suffering? It is the noble Eightfold Path, namely: Right Understanding, Right Thought, Right Speech, Right bodily Action, Right Livelihood, Right Effort, Right Mindfulness and Right Concentration.

Before we go further, let me explain the Noble Eightfold Path according to *A Manual for Buddhism*, a textbook of Buddhism used in the Sri Lankan primary schools (pp. 108f.).

1. Right Understanding is the knowledge of the Four Noble Truths. It is the understanding of oneself as one really is.

2. Right Thoughts are threefold:
    a) thoughts of renunciation which are opposed to lustful desires;
    b) benevolent thoughts which are opposed to illwill; and
    c) thoughts of harmlessness which are opposed to cruelty.

3. Right Speech deals with refraining from falsehood, slandering harsh words and frivolous talk.

4. Right bodily Action deals with refraining from killing, stealing and unchastity.

5. Right Livelihood deals with the five kinds of trade which should be avoided by a lay disciple; trading in
    a) arms,
    b) human beings,
    c) flesh (that is, breeding animals for slaughter),
    d) intoxicating drinks, and
    e) poison.

6. Right Effort is fourfold:
    a) the endeavour to discard evil that has already arisen;
    b) the endeavour to prevent the arising of unrisen evil;
    c) the endeavour to develop unrisen good; and
    d) the endeavour to promote that good which has already arisen.

7. Right Mindfulness is fourfold: Mindfulness with regard to
    a) body,
    b) sensation,
    c) mind, and
    d) phenomena.

8. Right Concentration is the one-pointedness of the mind.

This is the whole message of Buddhism. I am proud of the Buddha. (I may be violating the 'Right Speech' but it gives me a special joy to know that he was an Asian!) I thank God for giving these words of wisdom to millions of Asians through this man Siddhattha Gotama. 'in past generations he allowed all the nations to walk in their own ways; yet he did not leave himself without wit-

82

ness...' (Acts 14:16-17). Sorry to say, however, that the Four Noble Truths have been largely ignored and not really appreciated. The historical manifestation of Buddhism as a religion, its hierarchical structure, its power struggle, its expensive temples, its history of complicated cultural assimilation, hindered the masses in coming directly to the wisdom of the Four Noble Truths. Just as Christianity as a historical religion has hindered many people in coming to Jesus Christ, so it has been with Buddhism.

I think people should take time to meditate upon these words of the Buddha's. It is amazing how illuminating the Four Noble Truths are to our life today. This recommendation is particularly directed to the Asian Christians who are often cultural cripples. We Asian Christians ignore our own cultural heritage: arts, literature, painting, poetry, religious and historical experiences. Frequently, the moment of baptism becomes the moment of 'becoming a stranger' to one's own cultural and religious values. It is not so much due to one's faith in Jesus Christ, but one's acceptance of another (American, British, German ... the West's) way of life as the Christian way. What a misunderstanding!

A strange and positively unhealthy element has crept into the piety of Asian Christians. We think that if we speak well of the Buddha, admiring him for profound wisdom and penetrating observation, we are not loyal to Jesus Christ, or even, we are committing the grievous act of apostasy! Saying something affirmative about the Buddha is auto-

83

matically understood as saying something negative about Jesus Christ. That is to say, in order to magnify Jesus Christ one must speak disapprovingly about all other great sages. This reminds me of the cheapest kind of commercial battle in which the quality of one brand of washing powder is maintained only by pointing out the defects of others. That just shows how desperate we are to find goodness in Jesus Christ. If we do this we are insulting Jesus Christ, the Head of the Church and the universe (Colossians 1:15-20). Isn't it true that we are speaking of Jesus Christ in the same way that an inferior washing powder is advertised?

> Finally, brethren, whatever is true, whatever is honourable, whatever is just, whatever is pure, whatever is lovely, whatever is gracious, if there is any excellence, if there is anything worthy of praise, think about these things. Philippians 4:8

instant-salvation religion and at-that-moment-salvation religion

According to the Japanese Ministry of Education there were one hundred and thirty-six new religions and sects registered in the year 1947. In 1949 it was said there was 'one new religion every seven days'. In 1951, four hundred and ninety new religions and sects were created. Most of these 'new religions' were instant religions, promising instant material and spiritual gains. Some of them appealed unashamedly to the 'hitting-the-lottery psychology' of the people. These instant religions promised instant salvation by suggesting how to *use* gods for man's happiness.

In contrast to these new post-war instant religions of Japan, the world in the last two thousand five hundred years has known five great historical (noninstant) religions; three came from the Near East (Judaism, Christianity and Islam) and two originated in India (Hinduism and Buddhism). These great religions have lived with people for centuries and are actively influencing the minds and spirits of millions of people today. The youngest of them, Islam, came into being through the Prophet Mohammed in the early seventh century A.D. Today Judaism has twelve million adherents, Christianity eight hundred and forty million, Islam four hundred million, Hinduism three hundred and thirty-six million and Buddhism one hundred and fifty-seven million.

Great religions are not 'instant' religions promising instant and cheap salvation. The salvation they proclaim cannot be obtained as one puts a coin in a Coca Cola machine and gets a bottle. There is no 'bargain sale' or 'automatic sales machine' of salvation in the great religions. 'Do not give dogs what is holy; and do not throw your pearls before swine, lest they trample them under foot and turn to attack you' (Matthew 7:6). Cheap salvation is a false salvation. Real salvation does cost something. Gautama Buddha achieved enlightenment only after tremendous self-renunciation and self-mortification. It is clear that his message of salvation does not come from a 'bargain sale counter'. The Buddha's message of salvation is proclaimed in his first sermon which is called *Dhammacakkappavattana Sutta*. This first sermon promises man no easy salvation. It demands radical self-denial. The Four Noble Truths is the central part of the first sermon.

Jesus Christ does not promise instant and cheap salvation.

> Then Jesus told his disciples, 'If any man would come after me, let him deny himself and take up his cross and follow me. For whoever would save his life will lose it, and whoever loses his life for my sake will find it...' Matthew 16:24-25

86

How about the life of the Apostle Paul? Salvation in Jesus Christ brought to him more intensified self-denial:

> To the present hour we hunger and thirst, we are ill-clad and buffeted and homeless, and we labour, working with our own hands. When reviled, we bless; when persecuted, we endure; when slandered, we try to conciliate; we have become, and are now, as the refuse of the world, the offscouring of all things. I Corinthians 4:11-13

In the history of the Christian Church, however, the holy tradition of costly salvation has often been eroded by a longing for cheap salvation. Martin Luther's Reformation in the sixteenth century began with exactly this problem. There was a sale of 'sin-forgiving certificates' (indulgences) authorized by the Church. The certificate was 'a spiritual cheque always made out in favour of a definite person, irrespective of whether he was among the dead or the living. In case he was dead, it immediately promoted the designated person from purgatory to heaven. In case he was still among the living and had made proper confession to the indulgence priest, it guaranteed him absolution from all temporal penalties for sin previously incurred, and hence also from the corresponding purgatorial punishments.' (H. Boehmer *Martin Luther: Road to Reformation* p.178) The theologian, John Tetzel, promoted the 'bargain sale' of salvation. Let me quote another paragraph from the same book (p.181):

> When he had finished his sermon, he would himself usually go to the indulgence chest and buy a certificate for his father or some other dead person, and when the money tinkled in the chest, he would cry out 'Now I am sure of his salvation, now I need pray for him no longer'. In this way he stirred up the people, 'especially the sentimental matrons', so that they too came to the chest and bought certificates.

87

The Gospel of Jesus Christ was controlled by 'the money tinkling in the chest'. In such a case man is not believing in God but using God.

It would be an exciting study to find in what ways the great historic religions do *not* teach cheap salvation. But that would be beyond the scope of this brief meditation. I must proceed. In the well-known parable of the 'Prodigal Son' the scene of the coming back of the son is movingly described as follows:

> And he arose and came to his father. But while he was yet at a distance, his father saw him and had compassion, and ran and embraced him and kissed him. And the son said to him, 'Father, I have sinned against heaven and before you; I am no longer worthy to be called your son.' But his father said to his servants, 'Bring quickly the best robe, and put it on him; and put a ring on his hand, and shoes on his feet; and bring the fatted calf and kill it, and let us eat and make merry; for this my son was dead, and is alive again; he was lost, and is found'. And they began to make merry. Luke 15:20-24

The son never expected that he would receive an instant salvation. 'I am no longer worthy to be called your son' he says. In coming back to his father's home, he was not light-hearted. He was serious. He prepared what he would say when he met his father and, in accordance with his own plan, he said it to his father. But before all this there was a waiting father. He saw the son 'at a distance'. He had compassion. He ran to the son, he embraced him, he kissed him, he gave orders to his servants to do what should be done on the occasion of the 'resurrection of the dead'. Robe, ring and shoes signify the sonship. Bring not just any calf, but a *fatted* calf! The waiting father embraced and kissed him. *At the moment of this kiss* the son was saved. This moment was the moment of salvation. It was not a kiss planted by a lazy or unconcerned father or by an insensitive father. It was the kiss of one who had suffered so much! It was the kiss of one who in a full measure had experienced the cost of separation ('this my son was dead'!) and the joy of reunion ('and is alive again'!). The story is not a superficial one. It is a deeply involved, spiritual story. The waiting father has gone through the agony of waiting. The moment of that kiss—not an ordinary kiss, but a kiss which sealed the joy of *reunion after separation*—was a costly moment. *At the moment* of this kiss the son was saved.

Read another famous story in Luke, the story of Zacchaeus, the chief tax collector (Luke 19:1-10):

> 'Behold, Lord, the half of my goods I give to the poor; and if I have defrauded any one of anything, I restore it fourfold.' And Jesus said to him, 'Today salvation has come to this house, since he also is a son of Abraham. For the Son of man came to seek and to save the lost'.

Zacchaeus expressed his faith in a tax collector's language. He thought he was waiting on the tree to see Jesus. But suddenly he found out that Jesus was waiting for him. This shook him. You remember that 'he made haste and came down, and received him joyfully'? *Today—at the moment* when the seeking Jesus found the lost Zacchaeus and Zacchaeus responded to this event in his own way— salvation has come! This moment began for him a new life.

> As he entered Capernaum, a centurion came forward to him, beseeching him and saying, 'Lord, my servant is lying paralyzed at home, in terrible distress'. And he said to him, 'I

will come and heal him'. But the centurion answered him, 'Lord, I am not worthy to have you come under my roof; but only say the word, and my servant will be healed. ...' When Jesus heard him, he marvelled, and said to those who followed him, 'Truly, I say to you, not even in Israel have I found such faith.' And to the centurion Jesus said, 'Go; be it done for you as you have believed'. And the servant was healed at that very moment. Matthew 8:5-13

This story is centred on the strong faith of the non-Jewish military officer. It is faith that produced new life 'at that very moment'. The story sounds like a Coca-Cola-machine salvation story. The military officer came to Jesus with his problem. Rather his problem pushed him to come to Jesus. He might have been looking for an instant-salvation. He might have wanted to *use* Jesus' healing power to solve his personal problem ('my servant is lying paralyzed at home, in terrible distress'). In the world of the Bible it is the meeting of God and man in faith that brings forth the moment of salvation. *It is the meeting, not the using.* In the meeting between God and man, God's salvation comes 'at that very moment'. In the *using* of God for man's advantage arise all dangerous religions-of-instant-salvation which are not really salvation. Jesus saw the faith of the military officer. He saw that military officer was not using him but meeting him in faith. *Jesus made this distinction.* '...Jesus heard him, he marvelled ...' The story of this military officer was not a Coca-Cola-machine salvation story.

To come to God in faith (the meeting between God and man) is not all automatic. Each meeting takes place within a painful and real story. The Biblical faith prohibits using God. It is not a cheap-instant-

90

salvation religion. But it *is* a costly at-that-moment-salvation religion.

eyebrow controversy

Thailand is a strong Buddhist country. There are 240,000 Buddhist monks in the kingdom. They wear saffron robes and live simply in the temple dormitories. They are the living expression of the doctrine of the Buddha.

A monk shaves off his eyebrows. This makes his face more subdued—less expressive, less 'colourful', less 'busy' and less 'noisy'. It does indeed make quite a difference! Until I studied the face of a monk I did not realize how important eyebrows are! We use them to communicate the mood of our mind to others by raising or lowering them, contracting them or stretching them. Beauticians are quick to make use of these wonderful eyebrows commercially in order to make a million dollars. They suggest: shave them off (so far like the Buddhist monks), then paint on more expressive, longer and colourful ones (very anti-Buddhistic). And how is this done? 'Use our brush and paints.' Who can compete with this quick business acumen?

Why do Buddhist monks shave off their eyebrows? It is to show that they are men dedicated to the ideal of 'colourlessness', 'emptiness' and 'quietude'. They long to achieve *Nirvana*, the ultimate extinction and nothingness. In *Nirvana*, nothing is raised and lowered, wrinkled or stretched. It is the 'land of the radiant smile with nobody smiling' as the Thai monk Buddhadasa says. The face without eyebrows expresses the foretaste of the promised bliss of absolute quietude and emptiness.

The moment a monk shaves off his eyebrows he publicly confesses his religious commitment. It is a tremendous symbolic act comparable perhaps to the Christian baptism. When a woman shaves off her beautiful eyebrows she is doing it, I am sure, out of her conviction that painted eyebrows would be much prettier than her own. This is not a symbolic act. It is an act of 'shallow' and immediate significance. It makes, of course, beauticians happy since their bank accounts swell. Beauticians like Helena Rubinstein replace something superior by something inferior, and by doing this make fantastic incomes!

The Buddha stands opposed to this kind of vicious operation. He calls Man's attention to the final cause of human suffering. He tells us the way of liberation from suffering. Liberation is in the life of *detachment*. As long as a woman is attached to the eyebrows she had when she was eighteen years old, she is bound to feel sad when she sees her forty-year-old eyebrows! Where there is attachment, there is sorrow. The Buddha says 'accept the fact

that you are now forty, and keep yourself safe
from falling into a hopeless, vicious process which
will beget more and more sorrows.' Helena Rubinstein says, 'do not accept that you are forty years
old. You can become eighteen again. Our magic
brush and paint will make you stunningly attractive.'

Helena Rubinstein has tremendous money power
to advertise her products. The Buddha has no advertising firms backing his idea. Anyone who walks
on the streets of Bangkok can see that Helena
Rubinstein has won the battle over the eternal wisdom of the Buddha. Let us have more discussion
between Helena Rubinstein and the Buddha in the
minds of the Thai people.

> Let not yours be the outward adorning with braiding of hair,
> decoration of gold, and wearing of robes, but let it be the hid-
> den person of the heart with the imperishable jewel of a gentle
> and quiet spirit, which in God's sight is very precious. I Peter
> 3:3-4

94

cinema advertisements

Have you seen advertisements on the big cinema
screen? Of course you have. Our life today is satu-
rated with advertisements: cigarettes, beer, wine,
soap, wigs, cameras, motor-cycles, cars, radios, cos-
metics, devices to give you a more shapely figure,
tourism, etc., etc., ... Ideal men and women—young
beautiful and healthy—are portrayed using these
'wonderful things'. A 7-Up advertisement is a high
action picture of a group of young men and women
in a speed boat zooming over the blue sea. As they
zoom they drink 7-Ups. A young couple in love
board a London-bound BOAC jet. A beautiful Chinese girl takes a hot shower using the most delicate-
ly perfumed soap imaginable. Rugged young fel-
lows smoke cigarettes on horseback. We are forced
to see these 'ideal scenes' wherever we are and
wherever we go. We do not know how much we
are controlled by the ever-present persuasion of advertisements.

Advertisements are failures if they do not attract
attention and interest us. The sole mission of any
advertisement is to make people aware of the goods,

covet them and buy them. In order to do so, 'ideal scenes' are important. What are the ingredients, so to speak, of these ideal scenes? They are roughly *speed, youth, beauty, convenience* and *dreams*. When these five elements are combined ideal scenes can be produced.

A camera? Take a *young, beautiful* woman, put her in a sleek open car with a handsome young man at the wheel, and send them *speeding* along a lovely country road. Then *without any inconvenience* at all (adjusting lens, measuring light) she snaps a perfect picture. This is not something everyone can do *(dream)*! It is too good to be true. But the whole sequence gives one an impression that if you buy a camera—a car, a beautiful girl, and lovely surroundings will come free of charge! Yes. It will all be yours ... if you buy this camera!

Let me say a few words about 'dreams'. Isn't it true that very few of us have the chance (financial capability) of boarding a London-bound jet just for relaxation and vacation? Isn't it true that very few of us can have the enviable chance of drinking 7-Ups in a zooming speed boat? How many of us have smoked cigarettes on horseback while rounding up cattle in the vast prairies? Does every girl have an ideal figure which makes the soap she uses become by necessity ideal soap? The answers seem to be negative. These scenes are all 'dreams'. They are 'wish-fulfilling' or 'substituting' performances. I am smoking in a dirty crowded room—there are no horses or cattle around. But remember that healthy fellow! He does what I wish I could do. He does it for me! I 'dream' him. How can cigarettes be hazardous to my health? Look at my strong hero on horseback!

The falsity of these ideal scenes becomes clearer when one listens to the commentator's captivating voice. He does not speak the language as it is spoken every day. He speaks in a carefree voice. It is the voice of a seducer. We receive it, not through our ears but through our bellies. What he says in this sense is neither intelligent nor rational. It is intended to woo the audience with smooth talk. In cinema advertisements to be 'ideal' is to be 'carefree' and to be 'smooth'. Here is a girl suffering from pimples on her face. As far as she is concerned this is a matter of greater importance than nuclear warfare. She is friendless and dull. But behold! in a fraction of a second her skin becomes as beautiful and clear as Elizabeth Taylor's. The magic cream (cold cream or hot cream, I forget!) did the trick. Now she is alive, popular and all smiles. She is saved. It is quite obvious that this is a lie. But it is a 'truth' for the pimple-faced girl. It is a message of salvation long awaited. This 'truth' has to be explained quite legitimately and understandably by the voice of the seducer. So the commentator does a remarkable job of manipulating his voice so that the 'truth' will be received in her dreaming mind without being questioned. Suppose the advertiser was questioned later about the honesty involved in this matter he would only need to answer (either yes or no—it doesn't make any difference either way) in the seducer's voice. It is not the seducer but the one who listens to him who is found guilty.

Normally when a man or woman reaches forty years of age he or she begins to look at things differently (I hope). Speed, youth, beauty, convenience and dreams are given critical appraisal. Most advertisements therefore lose their punch when directed at older people, or, we may even say that most advertisements ignore the older generation except as they are enticed to be 'young again'. They concentrate on the 'up to thirty' age group. And if a person happens to be uncritical, immature, gullible, then he voluntarily includes himself in this group, even though he may be fifty. This gives the advertiser an extra bonus!

> 'Beloved, do not believe every spirit, but test the spirits to see whether they are of God, ...' I John 4:1

eat as much as you can!

Let's eat! Just look at this advertisement:

From 7 p.m. tomorrow you can have a big feast of the most exotic Cantonese and Szechuan dishes. More than 30 varieties prepared right under your very eyes.

EAT AS MUCH AS YOU CAN of as many varieties as you like.

Come alone if you have to. Otherwise come in a party of eight and we'll throw in a steam boat. On the house.

And after your feast we will not upset you with a 10% service charge.

Chilli Crabs
Steamed Prawns
Chicken With Dry Pepper
Fried String Beans
Fried Prawns With Chilli Sauce
Fried Beancurd Country Style
Frogs Legs With Pepper Sauce
Hainan Chicken Rice
Shredded Chicken With
    Chilli Sauce and Seaweed
Braised Abalone and
    Asparagus
Preserved Eggs With Ginger
Fried Pork
Roasted Duck
Roasted Chicken
Penang Ken Chai Boey
Braised Seaslugs With Lotus
    Seeds
Braised Tendor With Brown
    Sauce
Roasted Pigeon
Fried Prawns Rolled in
    Seaweed
Stewed Mixed Vegetables
    Deluxe
Fried Noodles
Fried Rice and White Rice

Curry Chicken
Steam Boat
Szechuan Pastry
Chinese Pancake
Salted Szechuan Pastry With
    Meat
Roasted Bread (Ban Toh)
Silver Roll
Papaya
Fruits and Fruit Salad in
    Water
Melon
Almond Beancurd With Lychee

I read the list of delicacies carefully and say to my-self again and again, 'Eat as much as you can!', 'Eat as much as you can'! Isn't this a generous offer at £1.00? I can dine like a Roman Emperor savouring exotic dishes from the far corners of the world! Am I hungry? Of course, I am. No, I don't mean hungry in the sense that I have not had a decent meal lately. In fact, I have been eating well. To tell you the truth, I am overweight. (Probably my stomach would welcome a lighter diet!) but I do enjoy eating out, particularly with good friends. 'Eat as much as you can'! I love this 'no limit' idea, the suggestion that I can stop or go on as I please. *It makes me feel free.*

All day long I am aware of the pressures upon me and the many limits I must not or cannot exceed. As a businessman I make decisions, but they are guided by my present state of business financial backing, anticipated events and personal involvement. As a father I know the limitations of my family—my son will not be a brilliant scientist, nor my daughter a ballerina; my wife is not the most sophisticated hostess; and I am not (I must admit) the shrewdest merchant.

'Eat as much as you can'! I was wondering what to do this evening when I saw this advertisement. 'Frogs legs with pepper sauce' and 'Szechuan pastry' certainly sound delicious! Not that frogs legs really tempt me that much—what really attracts me is the idea of 'eating as much as I can' of as many varieties as I like. The thought is tantalizing. I won't be satisfied until I have the experience.

big waste, small waste

Now when Jesus was at Bethany in the house of Simon the leper, a woman, came up to him with an alabaster jar of very expensive ointment, and she poured it on his head, as he sat at table. But when the disciples saw it, they were indignant, saying, 'Why this waste? For this ointment might have been sold for a large sum, and given to the poor.' Matthew 26:6-9

Our world is frustrated. Ours is the day of 'global frustration'. Each one of us, without exception, experiences this frustration. Mankind today is spending £6 billion a year on armaments! (The United Methodist Church spends approximately £7,400,000 on overseas work.) The world is loaded with gunpowder. It is said that there are fourteen and a half tons of TNT to each person on earth today. We *waste* money on a fantastic scale. Being aware of this, if we are not frustrated, something is definitely wrong with us. Why do we waste so much? And even take pleasure in wasting? Is it because we forget how to 'waste' the costly ointment on the head of the Anointed One? Were the disciples right when they said 'Why this waste? For this ointment might have been sold for a large sum, and given to the poor'? But money is not going to the poor! It is going to armaments (a gigantic waste?). A small 'waste' is chided in order to save money for a gigantic 'waste'? Isn't this what we are witnessing today? If we really know how to 'waste' in the practice of 'love your neighbour' we may not have to waste our substance on a cosmic scale. But we find it particularly difficult to 'waste' anything for the sake of 'love'. Yet we are always ready to waste enormous amounts for the purpose of destruction. Doesn't this show how theological our frustration is?

helicopter history?

History! What is history? 'History' is a word familiar to all of us. There are thousands of history books—'History of South East Asia', 'History of Hong Kong', 'History of Modern Japan', 'History of the World's Great Civilizations', 'History of Islam', 'History of Christianity' and so on. Each one of us has a history. I was born in Tokyo of Japanese parents in 1929—that event begins my personal history. History is a story; not a fairy story like Cinderella or Snow White. It is a true story of the world, a nation, a community and individuals—a story which always involves people. History is personal. It is not mechanical. It is not systematic. It is neither neat nor clean. That is why history is so interesting. A textbook on history is, strictly speaking, impossible. A personal story cannot become a 'textbook'. History is a 'lived' story, and it is the 'living' that brings out meaningful thoughts for our present life experience. History does not just speak of the past but is also concerned about the present.

History is appreciated, quite obviously, by the *present* man, not the *past* man. The event of Exodus cannot be appreciated by the Pharoah in 1975; he has been dead a long time! We appreciate it, making it speak to us in our own situation. (Of course we know how deeply the past has influenced the present.) History can only be viewed from the present. It becomes meaningful only to the present. The present is the first breath of life-giving oxygen to make history alive for our use. This is the priority the present has in its relationship to history.

The helicopter approach to history means that we are carried back over the hundreds of years of history-terrain to the farthest point where we are dropped to begin our study. Applying this method to Church History means taking the helicopter back over two thousand years and being put down in apostolic times to begin the walk back to the twentieth century. This is the way most of us have been taught Church History, in fact this helicopter approach has been understood as the only possible approach. I see, of course, great value in this, but it does not, however, make history as interesting as in reality it is. This chronological approach tames history for our present use. History is a story-in-sequence. True, but it is more 'wild', more energetic than a systematic 'story-in-sequence'. The second century follows the first century and the third comes next. If I were to say that Luther's Reformation came before Augustine, I would be wrong. That Augustine came first is an historical fact. But how much weight should be given to 'chronological orientation' of history-understanding? Just how important is it? I am not suggesting that we should ignore the chronological helicopter approach but I do not think that this is the only possible approach to history. The helicopter approach has unfortunately made the study of Church History boring for our Asian students. Asians are put down in first-century Palestine where their study begins. Since the main stage of the drama is set in the West—I personally lament over the historical facts that Saint Augustine was not an Indonesian, Luther not a Chinese, Kant not a Burmese, Pope Paul not a Filipino—students acquire mostly 'Western' Church History. But all the time

2,000 years

the great story of the history of Asian nations, their civilizations and cultures were ignored. A tremendous wealth of Asian historical experience is overlooked by the Asians! In view of this I would like to suggest the 'riverboat' approach. Like the riverboats in Sarawak which go upstream for days at a time, approach Church History from our Asian 1975 situation and work backwards. Then in order to pick up relevant material from various parts of history, both East and West, I would suggest that the 'riverboat' approach go hand in hand with the *'smorgasbord'* approach. History is such a rich variety of food from which we can choose. A combination of the three approaches—helicopter, riverboat and *smorgasbord*—would not perhaps be powerful enough to penetrate into history, but students would be assured of a more interesting and rewarding experience by delving into history with this combination.

undomesticated god

The religion of the Old Testament begins without any building. And it is always somewhat suspicious of buildings being erected.

The first building project was Noah's 'three-storey Ark' (Genesis 6:15-16). But it was obviously a temporary arrangement for the limited time of the flood. 'So Noah went forth and his sons and his wife and his sons' wives with him. And every beast, every creeping thing, and every bird, everything that moves upon the earth, went forth by families out of the ark.' (Genesis 8:18-19). That was the end of the ark and it was abandoned. What a waste of material! This clean end is, as I see it, in accordance with the spirit of the biblical faith.

Then comes the famous story of the Tower of Babel: 'Then they said, "Come, let us build ourselves a city, and a tower with its top in the heavens, and let us make a name for ourselves, lest we be scattered abroad upon the face of the whole earth".' (Genesis 11:4). God was obviously not happy with the arrogant idea behind this building programme, 'a tower with its top in the heavens'. The basis of the biblical faith is not that man goes up to God but that God comes down to man. So God 'confused the language of all the earth' (v.9).

The 'lasting' (and enormously expensive) building of the Old Testament was the temple built in Jerusalem by Solomon. The idea of building a temple to God—the God of Exodus!—was not native to the people of Israel. In fact the temple itself was designed by Canaanite architects and it shows clearly the invasion of the Canaanite culture into the heart of the nomadic religion of Israel. The construction involved tremendous expenses and a huge labour force. Solomon harshly exploited people as the Pharaohs of Egypt had exploited their subjects, a practice obviously condemned by the Biblical writers. Solomon's 'lasting' temple was plundered and burned by the Babylonians in 586 B.C. and out of

the ruins the second temple was built in 515 B.C. This second temple stood nearly five hundred years and was superseded by Herod's temple which was devastated by the Roman soldiers of Emperor Titus in A.D. 70. In A.D. 136 Emperor Hadrian erected a temple to Jupiter Capitolinus on the site of the temple, and in A.D. 691 'Abd-al-Malik' built the Islamic 'Dome of the Rock' on the site.

The biblical tradition was always keenly aware of the danger of 'temple religion' for man becomes attached to the temple 'made by men' (Acts 17:24) and wilfully ignores the fact that God is free in his work of love outside and beyond 'sacred buildings'. The freedom of God, even though it means the freedom of the love of God, does not make man happy. Man wants to control and domesticate God. Man wants to confine God in some definite place. He puts God in a cage, as it were, with inspiring ceremonies and praises! God is thus 'grounded' (localized) in the temple and this arrangement gives man an opportunity to commercialize his grace. Special 'sacred persons' are assigned to the temple to retail and distribute the 'tamed' grace of God to the people. This is the way stingy man handles a generous God! (Matthew 20:15). Soon this temple arrangement of God's saving activity becomes so central that a vicious and subtle exchange (Romans 1:25) between God himself and the temple takes place.

Attachment to a 'sacred temple' can produce an extraordinary lie! Jeremiah saw this: 'Do not trust in these deceptive words: "This is the temple of the

110

Lord, the temple of the Lord, the temple of the Lord".' (Jeremiah 7:4). Note also this terrible reaction of Jesus: 'And as he came out of the temple, one of his disciples said to him, "Look, Teacher, what wonderful stones and what wonderful buildings!" And Jesus said to him, "Do you see these great buildings? There will not be left here one stone upon another, that will not be thrown down".' (Mark 13:1-2).

Jesus Christ ascended into heaven. And the Holy Spirit came. The Spirit of Jesus Christ is as much present in Tokyo, Peking and Jakarta as in Jerusalem and Antioch. His Spirit is present everywhere, there is no 'overseas missionary' work in his scheme as though a certain locality can be the centre from which mission can go out 'overseas'. The presence of God is no longer localized except '...where two or three are gathered in my name, there am I in the midst of them' (Matthew 18:20).

russian old women

Zagorsk *Troitsa* (Trinity) Monastery is about forty miles outside Moscow. It was founded by the most beloved Russian mystic monk Saint Sergius in the fourteenth century. He died in 1392. It became the centre of the monastic movement in Russia throughout the centuries. The residence of the Moscow Patriarchate is there within the monastery walls. The onion-shaped domes of the chapels fall impressively on the visitors' eyes. The working committee of the World Council's Commission on Faith and Order met there in August 1973. We were accommodated in the guest house. It was a simple building but quite adequate and comfortable.

Russian food is, of course, quite different from Japanese food. We were extremely well fed. We ate a lot of smoked fish and caviar with raw tomatoes and cucumber. They go together well. I shall not forget the generous Russian hospitality we enjoyed there.

Zagorsk is open to anyone. All day long a stream of visitors comes from the neighbouring towns and even far off places. At any one time twenty or more tourist buses are parked outside the monastery. It is good to see people in the monastery compound. Certain sections, however, are restricted to the visitors. Sitting on one of the benches under a tree in the late afternoon I saw all kinds of ordinary Russian people; young children with their parents, young people, middle-aged men and women, old people and the crippled coming to seek healing from Saint Sergius.

Zagorsk Monastery must be for some people an important historical spot to visit, and for others a place of divine worship. The service of worship is going on continuously in one or other of the several chapels. The Monastery Church service on Sunday is packed and overflows. Impressive Russian choir singing is heard all through the three-hour service. All the people stand. I saw many, indeed many, old women there. *Russian old women.*

Russian old women. Of course, I have seen old women before. My mother is an old woman. I have seen English old women, American old women, German old women, Chinese old women, Malay old women, ... I stood among the Russian old women in the worship service. Streaks of morning sunshine were coming through the small windows. The crowded church was poorly ventilated. I am not a tall man. Yet my head was above the heads of the old women. They cover their heads with pieces of cloth. I looked around. Old women made up perhaps seventy per cent of the congregation, their faces small, their stature short and shrunken. Their backs bent. Many of them leaning upon canes. Old brown socks showed through the holes in their boots. Their eyes were dim, their teeth broken and scarce. Their ears perhaps no longer sensitive to sound, their minds no longer keen and alert. They looked tired. Yet they must have strong hearts—cholesterol-free hearts. They have worked for fifty years, day and night, to eke out a living for their families. They have provided warm homes in the long severe winters of Russia. The rough knuckles of their hands tell of labours of all kinds; washing in the ice-cold water, cutting wood, mending clothes, and what else? ...

I was surrounded by them. I looked at them. I forgot what was going on at the altar. The choir was singing and priests were appearing and disappearing. Russian old women were with me. As I watched them, I began to feel that I was surrounded by many 'Dostoyevsky stories'. They appeared to be at least seventy years of age. Some of them must have been over eighty. (Their diet must have been quite a simple one. They must have worked hard. Yet they remained healthy. Simple diet and hard work have kept them healthy. A very timely warning to the western world!) They have lived through a period of great change in the history of Russia. The Bolshevik Revolution led by Lenin which terminated the rule of the Czar took place in 1917. Their brothers, lovers and husbands must have been participants in this great social upheaval. The Second World War was another time of severe trial for the Soviet people. The war cost millions of Russian lives. Many of them must have lost sons at this time.

Yet, they have survived through all this. And they are today right next to me in this Zagorsk divine service! I have not means to find out their life stories. But looking at them I am moved. I begin to see the *beauty* of them, an intensely inspiring beauty! Their beauty is not that of an eighteen-year-old girl. Their beauty is spiritual and not physical. It is a beauty of sweat and not powder. It is a 'deep', not 'shallow', beauty. It is the beauty that shines through the experience of having lived out life against all sorrows and hardships.

Somehow I noticed the similarity between their beauty and the 'beauty' of Isaiah 53:2:

> For he grew up before him like a young plant, and like a root out of dry ground; he had no form or comeliness that we should look at him, and no beauty that we should desire him.

This 'no beauty' is the power which makes the 'not-beautiful' (shallow beauty, commercialized beauty) genuinely 'beautiful' (the beauty which bestows energy and meaning to human life and community).

> Let not yours be the outward adorning with braiding of hair, decoration of gold, and wearing of robes, but let it be the hidden person of the heart with the imperishable jewel of a gentle and quiet spirit, which in God's sight is very precious. I Peter 3:3-4

icons in the chapel
and icons in the museum

Zagorsk Monastery is one of the major centres of the Russian Orthodox Faith in the Soviet Union today. The Soviet government obviously does not suppress the Faith altogether, although it is apparent that it looks at the Church negatively. In the compound of the Monastery there are some twelve buildings: chapels, guest houses, theological school buildings, a museum and Patriarchate Office and Residence. The museum comes under the supervision of the government. Visitors are met by a government official at the entrance of the museum while elsewhere they are met by black-robed, bearded monks.

There are two sections in the museum. One section contains the collection of all kinds of Russian articles from the past and present: clothing, kitchen utensils, household objects, building-models and so on. The second section is a rare collection of a great number of historic icons housed in ten rooms adjacent to the first section. This icon section is not open to the public. Since we were there at the invitation of the Russian Orthodox Church a special permit was granted for us to view them. All of us were overwhelmed by the richness of the collection and the beauty of the icons.

The word *icon* derives from the Greek word *eikon*, meaning an image, figure, likeness, representation, picture. In the tradition of the Orthodox Church, the Holy Icons are pictures of Christ, the Mother of God, and the Saints. Some of them are as small as three inches by four inches, or less. Others are as big as two feet by three feet. They are the works of the master painters and artisans of the devoted Orthodox Faith in the past. The use of icons in the Church was, after much dispute, permanently authorized by the Empress Theodora in 843. The settlement of 843 is remembered among the Orthodox Christians as 'The Triumph of Orthodoxy'.

What was the issue around which the dispute took place? The controversy was called the 'iconoclast controversy'. 'Iconoclast' means 'icon-smasher'. The dispute lasted for one hundred and twenty years starting from the early seventh century. The smashers said that icon veneration is idolatrous. Those who would use icons (iconodulists), on the other hand, argued that when the Christian venerates an icon by kissing it or prostrating himself before it, he is not committing idolatry since the icon is not an idol but a symbol. Expounding the central truth of the Christian faith, the incarnation of God in Jesus Christ, they reasoned that the incarnation means that God became a man, Jesus Christ, visible and tangible. Incarnation is not a ghostly presence.

117

Icon symbolizes tangibly the saving meaning of incarnation.

There are candles
burning in front
of the icons in the
chapel

but no candles burn in the museum

Thus actually the iconoclast controversy was a serious theological dispute involving the understanding
of the person of Jesus Christ. Yet, there will always
be a tightrope walk between the use of symbol and
the possibility of idolatry.

I do not expect that the old Russian women know
about the history of the iconoclast controversy. I
am sure that theological subtlety is far above their
heads. I do not think they understand the meaning of icon 'Christologically'. They are not theologians. Simply they venerate the icon. They kiss it
countless times. They prostrate before it. They
make the sign of the cross in front of it and bow
deeply at each making of the sign. There is no
question of symbolism and idolatry in their minds
as far as I can see. Icons at the Zagorsk Monastery
must be the *most* frequently kissed objects in the
whole world. The most loved and kissed woman in
the world cannot compete with one of those icons!

118

The icons in the chapel where people come are actively and continuously 'at work'. They are alive. They have no time to rest. They are most faithfully on duty all the time. They are exposed to the needs of the people right there. These icons are in the place where they are supposed to be. They have been kissed by thousands of people who expressed thousands of different spiritual and physical needs. The icons are silent. Their eyes are wide open. They are most available and effective 'pastoral counsellors'.

In a great contrast, the icons in the museum are inactive icons. No one kisses them. They are art objects. You may admire them but you do not venerate them. The museum is the place where one is asked to take distance (in kissing one cannot take distance!) from the displayed objects, and admire and study them. The museum icons are 'clean' since they are not *in touch* with the people. They are not functioning as 'pastoral counsellors'. Once they must have been in the front line of the ministry. But now they are retired in a quiet place. If we were to take one of them out to the chapel immediately it would find itself surrounded by the people ceaselessly kissing it and venerating it. It would surely become active again.

In the museum there is no problem of symbolism and idolatry since there people look at icons as religious art. They may be profoundly inspiring but they are no more than religious art. In the museum the dimension of worship does not come in. Therefore we are freed from the discussion of symbolism and idolatry. In the chapel, strangely again, there is no *concrete* problem of symbolism and idolatry. As far as I can see, such theological discussion is far too sophisticated for most of the people. *Religious life is richly going on.* As usual perhaps, only theologians get nervous in the chapel.

life knowledge

I remember the surprised expression on a five-year old's face when I told him his heart was a pump which never stopped working, even when he was asleep. The wonderful truth was that his circulation system (and all other systems) worked well without his even knowing one of the most basic things a-bout his body. It worked independently from knowledge. His life neither began nor stopped because of his ignorance. Information and knowledge came later. Obviously, if life began to work only when we understood it then none of us would be living today. Actually, isn't it true, with the exception of medical doctors (and even they confess their 'learned ignorance'!) we live our lives without understanding how the intricate systems of our own bodies work? The surprise expressed by the child at his discovery was a symbolic event. This surprise is repeated throughout our lives as we discover more and more about ourselves.

May I say that life precedes knowledge? In other words 'there is something going on before we know and understand it'. But this 'something going

intricate
heart

working all
the time!

on before we know it' often comes to me as a comforting thought. I feel I am rooted and supported. I feel that I am something more than what I understand. I come to know that knowledge is not everything. And to know this is comforting.

'In the beginning was the Word' (John 1:1). Obviously, none of us knows what was 'in the beginning' simply because we were not there then. 'In the beginning' means, in an emphatic sense, 'in the time when something was there even before we knew anything about it!' So I understand this famous passage of the Gospel of John to mean that at that time of which we do not even have any understanding, there was already something going on. That something is the firm and comforting promise of God for man. Since 'in the beginning' also means 'at the foundation of', let me try and put it another way: at the foundation of our lives there is already working the life-giving promise of God for man.

God is life. He precedes our knowing of His life 'from the beginning'. But His life is going on 'at the foundation of our human lives'. If God's life

122

was not there or not activated until we came to know it, then we would never know it. We come to know it only because His Word was there 'in the beginning'. He goes ahead of us. 'And all the time the Lord went before them, by day a pillar of cloud to guide them on their journey by night a pillar of fire to give them light, so that they could travel night and day.' (Exodus 13:21).

Christian faith is a life-orientation. It involves, of course, knowledge. But this knowledge is a knowledge integrated in life-orientation. It is not a theoretical knowledge, but life-knowledge. Knowledge must be always humbled by the thought that there was already something going on—the purpose of God at the foundation of our lives—before we became aware of it.

'non'-christian?

Christians are often heard speaking of 'non-Christians'. For example: 'Mr A is now a Christian but he comes from a non-Christian family'; 'There are many millions of non-Christians in Asia'; 'Marriage between Christian and non-Christian'; 'Followers of the non-Christian religions'; 'Pakistan is a non-Christian nation'; 'Christian dialogue with non-Christians'. (And there are even such expressions as non-Methodist, non-Presbyterian, non-Evangelical). Obviously this is a convenient distinction. We regard all those who differ from ourselves as *nons*. We look at humanity as a whole, and then classify all those who are not Christians under the heading 'non-Christians'. It is as comprehensive as the sweeping distinctions between proletariat and bourgeois; free nations and the Communist world.

Who is a 'non-Christian'? One who has not been converted, not baptized, not a member of the church. Whether he is a Muslim, a Buddhist, a Hindu, a Marxist, rich or poor is of no account; what classifies him is his relation to Christianity—he is a non-Christian.

'Non-Christian' defines a man in terms of what he is not, not what he is. The label 'non-fat milk' on a can tells those of 'heart-attack' age an important message. 'Milk minus fat' is not a complex situation. By scientifically removing the fat from milk a product for the benefit of man is available. But labelling a person 'non-Christian' is quite different. People are not produced and processed in a factory. Everyone is an individual with his own awareness of *what he is*—not what he is not. *What he is* is full of imaginative ideas and experiences.

When we label a person as a non-Christian, we are looking at him as an object, negatively and arrogantly. No one can appreciate being viewed in this way—it is certainly not a healing action, but opens the wounds of division. It negates the very inclusive Christian love we are trying to teach. Nor is there any such static condition as non-Christian or Christian, as there is fat and non-fat milk. All are in movement because God rules.

> As they were going along the road, a man said to him, 'I will follow you wherever you go'. And Jesus said to him, 'Foxes have holes, and birds of the air have nests; but the Son of man has nowhere to lay his head'. To another he said, 'Follow me'. But he said, 'Lord, let me first go and bury my father'. But he said to him, 'leave the dead to bury their own dead; but as for you, go and proclaim the kingdom of God'. Another said, 'I will follow you, Lord; but let me first say farewell to those at my home'. Jesus said to him, 'No one who puts his hand to the plough and looks back is fit for the kingdom of God'. Luke 9:57-62

This is directed at all, irrespective of a label—Christian or non-Christian.

a drop in the bucket

REFUGEE RELIEF ACTION

The year 1971 saw the greatest exodus of human beings that has ever been recorded throughout all history. Ten million men, women and children left their homes and belongings in East Pakistan to flee across the borders into India. They fled from misery beyond our comprehension to live in primitive refugee camps spread around the borders. But however wretched their new existence in these camps it was still better than that from which they came.

Over a period of nine months, these 10 millions were spread throughout 1,000 camps. At the best these camps offered a bare minimum of food and shelter to an adult, but the lack of protein in the only diet available has been disastrous among children. Something like 2½ million children below the age of 8 are suffering from serious malnutrition. 150,000 of them have died already, and many more could die within the next few months. And this is in the camps where some organization prevailed. At border hospitals eyewitnesses have reported conditions of suffering so extreme that they almost defy description.

Now the refugees must return. This simple statement conceals a frightening potential for further disasters. Return to what? To an area that must be the poorest and most overpopulated in the world, at the best of times with a cereal food deficit of two million tons per year. But now it has seen natural disaster, war, and the confusion following a flight of ten millions.

There have been optimistic estimates of moving 100,000 people a day back across the borders ... but even at that rate it would take three months to shift ten million people. Independent observers who have visited the camps in the last week of 1971 say that a more realistic estimate of the time needed to rehabilitate the refugees would be from six to nine months. In the meantime these millions of unfortunate people will have to continue their desperate existence living under conditions which no human being should have to endure.

In the face of steady indifference of whole countries we believe as individuals that every effort to relieve such misery is of value. We are aware of the delicate political problems inherent in the situation but cannot accept that the immense human suffering involved should be ignored. Rising above all political involvement we wish to promote this campaign on purely humanitarian grounds and so avoid favouring any political attitude.

With this intent a committee has been formed to organize private subscriptions which will be administered in the refugee areas with the guarantee of the International Red Cross.

Souvenir Programme RRA Singapore

Ten million people have been made desperately destitute. Roughly thirty million in the region are hungry. How do you propose to feed fifteen times Singapore's population? Isn't it quite a job just to feed one hundred people? Chairs, tables, dishes, spoons, rice, fish ... to feed and clothe thirty million people—what a gigantic task!

What can Refugee Relief Action in Singapore do? Even if it did raise £150,000 it would literally be 'a drop in the bucket', yes, 'a tiny drop in a big bucket'! (in Japanese we say 'a drop of water dropped on the red hot stone'). When we realize that the need is on such a staggering scale, what meaning is there in a contribution of five, ten or twenty pounds? Let's be realistic. Only concerted efforts of nations (U.S.A., U.K., Germany, Soviet Union, Australia, Japan ...) can do the job. Quite true! Then should we stop Refugee Relief Action since its contribution would be 'a drop in the bucket'? 'A drop in the bucket' is the situation in which we

128

find ourselves and we are puzzled about what to do.

Help becomes help only when it carries a certain 'significant' size (quantity). 'A drop in the bucket' can hardly be of any help. 'A gallon in the bucket', on the other hand, makes sense. I understand this view. But no matter how insignificant *quantitatively* we must express our concern. Only by doing so can we maintain *qualitatively* our human-ness. To be human is not an automatic business. To be human means to show human concern over human need. We do not ask whether what we do amounts to 'a drop' or 'two drops' or 'one hundred drops'.

The Singapore RRA Committee organized lunches—the food being provided free by local Indian restaurants. The food was 'hot'. My stomach could not take it. But my heart understood the message. I said to myself: 'What an imaginative way to educate and raise money! Where does this unusual imagination come from?' It comes from a desire to help the refugees. That desire (love) made the RRA Committee imaginative. Where there is love there is creative imagination. Love is free to work under all circumstances. Love is not discouraged even when it knows that what it does amounts to 'a drop in the bucket'. Love does not puff up when it knows that what it does amounts to 'many gallons in a bucket'. Love has its own arithmetic. Theology concerns itself with the arithmetic of love. Arithmetic of love is called ethics.

happy communication

May I begin my talk with a big word—*communication*. Communication means to tell someone about something. Right now I am trying to tell you something. I am engaged in communication. All Singapore is so busy communicating that I am told the Telephone Board is changing all numbers to six-figure numbers. I understand this to mean that there is a tremendous need to increase telephone services in Singapore. Why do we need more telephones? Because we want to communicate with many people about many things as quickly as we can. On the third floor of the Bangkok Central Post Office there is the International Telephone Service. The other day I used it to speak to my office in Singapore. I paid 85 baht for three minutes. Today you can call practically all important cities of the world on the telephone.

I have spoken about the telephone but I am not advertising for the Telephone Board. The telephone does not need any advertisement. Everyone wants it. We all want to communicate. Communication is as basic to human life as blood. At the moment of birth, a baby makes a cry. 'Wa-ah, Wa-ah'. With this cry it communicates with its mother that it has arrived safely. Even before that the baby, still in its mother's body, made known to the mother and friends and relatives by kicking that it would soon come into the world! So, from before birth and continuously through life until the very moment of death we are busy communicating in every possible way. *To live is to communicate!* Just as we cannot live without blood, we cannot live without communication.

You may say that you have seen some people who don't speak to each other. They dislike each other so much they don't want to communicate with each other. You know this happens often between students and friends and even husband and wife. If this happens, in fact they are very much in communication! They are telling each other quite clearly that they don't like each other. So it is a strong communication! In all we do, in all we say, in all our movements, in all our actions and reactions, we are communicating. One way to stop communicating is to commit suicide. But remember that suicide is a very strong communication, too. A young women committed suicide recently and left a note to her husband: 'I hate you. You will be happy if I am dead!'

If communication is so important, we must take care of it. Isn't it true that we take special care of something that is important to us? If you have a motor cycle, don't you take care of it? Doesn't your

132

mother take care of you because you are important to her? Music is important to me, so I take care of my stereo set. So let's take care of our communication. But what does that mean?

We can say there are two kinds of communication: (1) business and (2) personal.

ARRIVING SINGAPORE FRIDAY SQ115 AT 1400 HOURS.

This is a business communication. A wife telling her husband that the April PUB bill was £7 is a business communication. The traffic policeman fining you because you drove your car too fast is a business communication. But 'I love you' is not a business communication; it is a personal communication. 'I like him (or her) because I feel somehow happy with him (or her). I wonder why it is so. Why do I like him and not that fellow over there? Why? I wonder.' This is a personal communication. Business communication is clear and to the point. Personal communication is not so clear. It is deeper and more complicated. In fact it is so deep and so complicated that none of us can really understand it.

You see the difference between business communication and personal communication? 'April PUB bill is £7' is a business communication. 'I love you' is a personal communication. 'I hate you' is also a personal communication. Now which do you like to hear from someone, 'I love you' or 'I hate you'? Do you like to hear someone tell you 'I hate you'?

If you do, you are not quite a normal person. Usually, we like to hear someone say to us 'I love you'. If your parents tell you so, don't you feel that it makes you contented and happy? Your parents or your friends do not exactly have to *say*, 'I love you'. They can indicate that they like you in many ways. I find that everyone, young and old, boys and girls, men and women, rich and poor, educated and un-educated, wants to be loved and not hated.

We all want to be liked and loved. So we try all kinds of things in order to realize this. There are so many cosmetic shops in Singapore. Obviously they do good business. Why? The girls buy lipsticks, nail varnish and so on. Why? They want to look beautiful. Why do they want to look beautiful; because they want to be liked. Liked by lipstick? No! liked by boys (other persons). Why do boys choose their trousers carefully? They want to look hand-some. Why do they want to look handsome? Because they want to be liked. Liked by trousers? No! liked by girls (other persons). We do all kinds of things with great effort in order to make people like us and love us. Lipstick and trousers are *not* our real concern. We are aiming to make people like us. That is our final goal.

But there is a strange thing in our world, too. We do all kinds of things to destroy others! We fight. We bomb. We kill. We say unkind things about each other. I said we do all kinds of things to make people like and love us. But it is also true that we do all kinds of things to make people dislike and hate us. How strange we are!

The question before everyone of us is this: How to increase love and how to decrease hate in our world. If this is the biggest and most important issue that faces us today, what can we do about it?

Now remember that we are always engaged in some kind of communication. To live is to communicate. To increase love and decrease hate in our world we must communicate love and not hate. It is rather obvious that we cannot increase love by communicating hate. We must communicate love. Yes. But what does that mean? I cannot give you a quick and easy answer. To find the answer is a life-long assignment which we must work at together. But you may permit me to make two brief observations on this.

(1) Business communication must not become the *whole* of your communication. Don't become a person who is *always* talking about business. That kind of life is abnormal, uninteresting, egocentric and unhappy. Personal communication is more important than business communication. Your personal communication will determine whether your life is to be a happy one or an unhappy one.

(2) Jesus said, 'I am the Way'. This is his personal communication. He meant 'I hope you will walk in the way of "I love you", and "I accept you".' 'I am with you. You are no longer lonely.' 'Don't be discouraged.' 'Hope.' 'Stand up and walk'. This is the most important communication we hear while we live. To remember this is to try to take care of our communication.

135

quite independently
of nagging

One thing we have learnt in relation to our children—and it has been a long hard lesson—is that continually reminding them of their failures in tidiness ('pick up your toys'), obedience ('go to bed it's eight o'clock'), cleanliness ('wash your face and brush your teeth'), honesty ('you said you wanted ice-cream and you bought coca cola!') simply does not achieve the desired effect. If we continue with this onslaught of nagging they may finally do as we want them to, but it will not be because they see value in doing so, but because we put them in a 'no exit' situation. We may have then, tidy, obedient, clean, honest children but they resemble robots more than human beings. The great human values—freedom and creativity—have been sacrificed.

Children are individuals with their own integrity when they reject tidiness, obedience, cleanliness and honesty. They are experimenting—something which robots cannot do. By saying this I do not mean that instructions are unnecessary. Children need to be reminded from time to time that they should put away their toys when they have finished with them. But I am convinced that the *bombardments* or *saturation bombing* approach to children, and for that matter to anyone, is wrong. It may reveal a lack of love. Love does not 'bomb' ceaselessly, on the contrary:

> Love is patient and kind; love is not jealous or boastful; it is not arrogant or rude. Love does not insist on its own way; it is not irritable or resentful—it does not rejoice at wrong, but rejoices in the right. Love bears all things, believes all things, hopes all things, endures all things. I Corinthians 13:4-7

Since fundamentally it is against a loving respect for the individual, constant nagging has only negative consequences pedagogically, psychologically, socially. It frustrates children, bores them, and gives them a wrong sense of social values. It produces an intolerable situation for the family.

Saturation bombing!—isn't this what happens at Sunday services? Sunday after Sunday we are told how unsatisfactory is our faith, how weak our commitment, how full of shortcomings we are in our practice of Christian living. Every Sunday we go to church to be scolded and chided. Fifty-two scoldings a year—five hundred and twenty in ten years—when scoldings are that frequent they become nagging. Our psychological reaction is basically similar to that of our children—boredom, frustration, confusion. As a result, churchgoers develop a special frame of mind for sixty minutes each Sunday, a defensive attitude. 'Let's not take this too seriously, after all the preacher is paid to nag us.'

One year has fifty-two Lord's Days, couldn't the preacher be more positive and refreshing at least

twenty-six times a year to make a balanced message? No, that's not good enough! Nagging has no
place in the Gospel of Jesus Christ. The Gospel is
the Gospel because it speaks of the immense mercy
and generosity of God in Jesus Christ.

> But now the righteousness of God has been manifested apart
> from the law, although the law and the prophets bear wit-
> ness to it, the righteousness of God through faith in Jesus
> Christ for all who believe. For there is no distinction; since
> all have sinned and fall short of the glory of God, they are jus-
> tified by his grace as a gift, through the redemption which is
> in Christ Jesus. Romans 3:21-24

'Apart from law'—I understand this to mean 'Apart
from nagging'.

italian-accent english in australia

The neighbourhood shopping area for the University of Melbourne is Carlton. There are three blocks of shops and stores along the main street. When you are tired of brain work at school, it is a nice place to walk around. One of the shops, Twin Hamburger, is run by Italian immigrants. Two grown-up men (twins) serve the customers. A whole broiled chicken is A$1.20. One of them says with a heavy accent, 'This chicken is guaranteed for three months!' Laughing, I felt salvation. Australia is an English-speaking country, but it is no longer a one-British-accent country. There are many accents coming in!

English is spoken with an Italian accent, Greek accent, Dutch accent, Egyptian accent, Yugoslavian accent... When I notice that English is being spoken with many different accents, I feel at home and 'saved'. I speak with a Japanese accent (it happens to be a heavy one!). Immigrants from European countries other than the British Isles are making Australian life colourful and culturally rich. Of

139

course, the country is still predominantly British in many ways. Yet there are non-British elements coming in rapidly. The Greeks brought in the tradition of the Greek Orthodox Church. This must be quite a new experience for Australia. In one section of Sydney which became heavily Greek a Methodist Church building was remodelled to be used by the Greek Orthodox. In Melbourne one sees a lot of Greek and Italian shopsigns.

When the people of different historical backgrounds live together—one must not be romantic about this sort of thing, because such an arrangement can sometimes produce serious tensions—that community is enriched. Enrichment and conflict come together. Marriage is an enrichment to the persons involved but it does not come free from conflict.

Chinese cuisine, 'sweet and sour pork' really can be sweet and sour at the same time. The co-existence of sweetness and sourness enriches the taste. Shallow enrichment of life may come without the experience of tension, but deeper and ultimately satisfactory enrichment would not come apart from conflict and tension.

I feel I stand out in Australia because I am Asian. Of course, I do not stand out at all in any part of Asia. I missed seeing Asians on the streets of the Australian cities. At times, I felt the Christian truth is, as it were, *lonely* there since it is not encountered by the presence of the Hindus, Muslims and Buddhists. The Christian truth does not have a 'sparring partner', to use a boxing image. The day may

140

come when Australia will have sizeable Muslim or Hindu communities. They will speak a different language to express their perception of the truth. Then will come a radical tension-enrichment situation.

Japanese make a sipping noise when they take soup. This would be regarded as quite impolite by English people. American people blow their noses in public, which Japanese, in turn, would think ill mannered. That which is different from our own is condemned without much thought. We are intolerant with the unfamiliar. We are tolerant with that which is familiar. There may be psychological reasons for this. We are generally afraid of anything which is unfamiliar. Our psychological defence mechanism (or perhaps our instinct) dictates to us that we must not go close to that which is unfamiliar lest we may be injured. We may make, therefore, a quick and premature judgement which is usually a negative pronouncement upon that which is unfamiliar, be it person, culture or way of doing things. Before I studied the Thai language, I could not understand how it was possible at all to do scientific investigation in the Thai language. I irrationally believed that only European languages *and* the Japanese language were equipped to engage in the communication of scientific research!

Human experience is limited. Even if a man goes around the world twenty times his 'world-experience' is limited. Man cannot become familiar with all things. To live with that which is unfamiliar is part of human destiny. And this destiny is a bles-

141

sing because it means that we live in the context of enrichment-conflict and conflict-enrichment. Our imagination soars and life is enriched when the unfamiliar is taken into our own human experience. English spoken with foreign accents in Australia is, then, an intensely significant event.

It seems to me that the world's history is moving towards an unprecedented and massive meeting of different cultures and peoples. No one is allowed to stand aside and take distance from this historical fact. 747 jets are continuously carrying all kinds of people in all directions. Thousands of students are studying abroad. Young people are marrying internationally. Television, newspapers and magazines are bombarding people with overseas news. Italian-accent English is spoken in Melbourne. This massive encounter among the peoples introduces enrichment-conflict situations. This, it seems to me, is where the world's history is heading. I see it taking place distinctively in Australia.

> And if you salute only your brethren, what more are you doing than others? Do not even the Gentiles do the same?
> Matthew 5:47

the spacious australia
and the mobile god

Geographically Australia is a huge country. It is 4,000 k.m. from east to west and 3,200 k.m. from north to south. To be exact, Australia has 7,686,420 sq. k.m. It is almost the same size as the United States excluding Alaska. About twenty Japans will make Australia. Yet, the whole Australian population is about that of Tokyo— 12,000,000 people! In terms of figures I am able to understand this spaciousness and small population of Australia. But it is another matter to spend a few months there and experience it.

Spaciousness is absolutely a positive value for human happiness. It is interesting that in Biblical language the idea of *salvation* contains the connotation of 'spaciousness'.

> Then the Lord said, 'I have seen the affliction of my people who are in Egypt, and have heard their cry because of their taskmasters; I know their sufferings, and I have come down to deliver them out of the hand of the Egyptians, and to bring them up out of that land to a good and broad land, a land flowing with milk and honey, ...' Exodus 3:7-8

Australia is a 'good and broad land'. Indeed, it is a 'super' good and broad land! I do not find a 'good and broad land'! I do not find 'a good and broad' space in the Tokyo underground. At peak hours it is murderously crowded. I fight for one inch of space. I fight for my life. Inside the train I fight for my salvation, but when I step out of the underground train on to the platform which is 'less crowded' I feel saved. I fix my tie at the right angle, straighten my coat, check my brief-case, then start walking as though I am a saved, new man. Being a Tokyo-man I have learned to appreciate the value of space.

'A good and broad land, a land flowing with milk and honey'—isn't this a concrete description of a salvation-land? Australia super spaciousness means, then, a super-salvation land. Spaciousness, however, does not automatically mean salvation. The land must be 'flowing with milk and honey'. The salvation must be 'spaciousness *plus* milk and honey'. Again, milk and honey do not flow automatically. Milk comes from cows. Honey comes from bees. Man must work to make 'milk and honey' flow. I have not yet seen milk and honey flowing by themselves. I can get them at milk bars! If the milk industry goes on strike, even though there are gallons and gallons of milk and honey it will not flow to the people's kitchens. Honey will not flow if transport is disrupted by petrol shortages or industrial disputes. Then to make 'milk and honey' flow is not as simple an operation as it seems at first glance. It involves complicated processes and planning. This fact was

144

demonstrated to the whole world with devastating clarity recently when the Arab oil stopped flowing. To make the oil flow again required worldwide complicated negotiations and reconciliation!

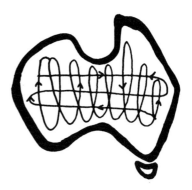

Sanctification of the space
by the presence of the
freely mobile holy God

Spaciousness must be an active spaciousness. It must not be a sleepy and lazy spaciousness. It must be an engaged spaciousness and not a deserted spaciousness. It must be a responsible spaciousness and not an irresponsible spaciousness. It must be cultivated spaciousness (cows and bees must be taken care of) and not an uncultivated spaciousness. Spaciousness must be blessed by both man and God. Man must realize the great potentiality of spaciousness. Spaciousness will become useful when man sees it as blessed by God, the Creator.

The Biblical God is the God of a moving and travelling people. He is not imprisoned in the temple. In his Temple Dedication prayer, King Solomon said:

> But will God dwell indeed with man on the earth? Behold, heaven and the highest heaven cannot contain Thee...
> II Chronicles 6:18

145

The temple is a symbol, just as a ring on the finger is the symbol of married status. That is why the destruction of the Temple of Jerusalem (A.D.70) has not destroyed the Jewish and Christian faiths. Our God is not a stationary God. Instead of man coming to God, God comes to man. Isn't this the point we are reminded of every year at the time of Christmas? 'And the Word became flesh and *tented* among us' (John 1:14). The tented Jesus Christ is mobile. He does not sit at one place. He comes to Zacchaeus. He comes to tax collectors. He comes to prostitutes. He comes to the lepers. He comes to the whole world! At his coming, saving events take place. Everytime? Yes. Strangely, they do! His coming has never been empty. Saving events come along with him. The reason for this is that He Himself is the greatest saving event.

The faith in this mobile God, the God who creates saving events—this faith is the faith that can bless, sanctify and baptize all sizes and forms of spaciousness. The mobile God (the tented Jesus Christ) means that spaciousness is always visited by this God. We are called to participate in this divine mobile visitation, to do the work of baptizing the spaciousness of Australia.

kangaroo and the hong kong – kowloon underwater tunnel

Congratulations! The new underwater road tunnel between Hong Kong and Kowloon has opened. Now traffic can travel in all weather at fifty miles an hour under the water. Unlike the ferry, it is fast and weather-free. You will 'come out on the other side' and you will not have seen a drop of water even though you have travelled under it. What progress! Suppose you are on the way to hospital in an emergency this tunnel may save your life! It is a blessing.

This tunnel was opened in August 1972, thirty-five months after work started. It was not a small project for the Hong Kong Government. The Cross-Harbour Tunnel Company commissioned a team of architects and engineers to plan the tunnel. These are the people who understand science and technology. They can solve difficult mathematical questions which are beyond our understanding. We must appreciate these people of science and technology. Without them no amount of money can give us this tunnel. They are the people who brought us this blessing.

Fifty miles an hour is fast. Man walks at three miles an hour. Race horses can run at forty-five miles an hour, greyhounds at forty miles an hour, and cheetahs at sixty-five miles an hour. But thanks to science and technology we can sit down comfortably in a car and go steadily at fifty miles an hour for hours if we wish. We can drive under the water in tunnels, and drive up mountains without sweat or exhaustion. How about jet aircraft? They can fly at six hundred miles an hour. The distance from Hong Kong to Singapore is covered in four hours. Singapore to Manila in three hours. Aeroplanes climb to an altitude of 35,000 feet and fly through the cold air of minus 50 degrees! We can enjoy a delicious meal and sip wine while we are flying.

We are living today in the world of 'speed above weather'. Remember winds and waves have nothing to do with the underwater tunnel. Remember that 'planes are above weather when they climb to 35,000 feet. Remember we can shut our car

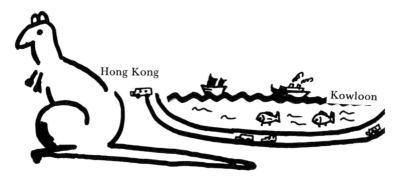

Hong Kong

Kowloon

windows in the rain and drive without getting wet. 'Speed above weather'—this is one of the oustanding marks of our civilization today. The Hong Kong-Kowloon tunnel is a powerful example of this.

Let me emphasize just one aspect of this 'speed-above-weather' style of man's mobility. It is this: when we walk (three miles an hour) we see many things, we notice many things, we feel wind, we feel rain, we are warmed by sunshine, we can smell the pleasant aroma as we pass food stalls, we may meet friends or even relatives. We hear children laugh and cry, and see them play. When we walk we see, feel, smell and hear so many interesting things. We are not shut up. We are not rushing at fifty miles an hour. Our pace is three miles an hour on our own feet. That is what makes this seeing, feeling, smelling and hearing possible.

When we see, feel, smell and hear people we are not lonely. Our life is enriched and encouraged. So beware of the 'speed-above-weather' style of life! It is a comfort and a blessing to us. But at the speed of fifty miles an hour can you see, feel, smell and hear people? You are isolated in the car, in a box on four wheels. In the car you do not have time to see, feel, smell and hear people. No! In fact you must not. All your attention must be on the road. Driving means 'do not hit people' (avoid people). Walking means 'meeting people' (be among people). The more speedy our life becomes the more 'lonely' we become! How strange this situation is! The blessing of science and technology makes the possibility of making man's life lonely and even impoverished very real.

If we go after mobility without thinking about our human relationships with others, then we will become like a kangaroo, with strong hind legs (mobility) and a small head (not much thought about human life and human value). What is needed is both strong legs (mobility) and a head (human relationships and enrichment deriving from them) in well-balanced proportions. Can you think of such an animal? Isn't man such an animal? Let's not deform man!

two kinds of typhoon

What fascinates me whenever I visit Hong Kong is the innumerable quantity of advertisements on the streets—the advertisements (some of them brightly lit neon signs after dark) are prominently displayed along the streets. They are all sizes, a variety of colours and in English and Chinese (and lately a good number have begun to appear in Japanese). As I step out of the Hotel Fortuna into Nathan Road and look in both directions I am surrounded by colourful advertisements. Double-decker buses pass along often skimming the protruding signs. Advertisements and more advertisements! 'Swiss watches', 'Sony Tape recorders', 'Sauna Bath', 'Peking Restaurant', 'Chinese Emporium', 'Books and Stationery', 'Night Club', 'Massage Parlour' and so on. Looking at them as I walk along I begin to feel as if I am walking through the yellow pages of a telephone directory!

Hong Kong is right in the main typhoon route. It is hit by a typhoon at least two or three times a year. Fifty miles an hour wind and torrential rain! The typhoon blows against these advertisements.

It damages them. It blows some of them one block away. Yet, as soon as the typhoon is over the signs are mended and put up again. This happens year in and year out. This makes me think that there must be some persistent and strong wind blowing within

our human minds counteracting the typhoon wind. A typhoon comes and damages the advertisements, but another kind of typhoon within us mends the advertisements and puts them up again. Another type of typhoon? Yes. In biblical language the word *spirit* comes from the word *wind*. Man has spirit. That is to say, then, man has *spiritual wind blowing within him*. And this 'inside' wind is very powerful, and it can blow at an incredible speed too! This 'inside wind' (another type of typhoon) comes from God. '... then the Lord God formed man of dust from the ground, and breathed into his nostrils the breath of life; and man became a living being' (Genesis 2:7). It was a good wind which made man alive, not just to exist. Man does not simply exist. Man lives. And he is supposed to live as God lives, a good happy and holy life.

As I walk along the Kowloon streets I feel many winds—'I-want-to-make-more-money wind', 'I-love-Peking-duck wind', 'I-want-to-have-a-massage wind', 'I-want-to-buy-this-or-that wind' ... I notice, in short, all kinds of 'I-want' winds blowing. These various winds blowing within us are not unrelated to each other. They are all related just as the winds that hit all streets and alleys come from one typhoon. All kinds of winds within man come from one *big wind* which is called an 'I-want-to-be-related-to-others wind' ... None of us wants to live alone. We need companionship. We want to have someone with whom we can share our lives. A life unshared is a sad and unfulfilled life. Eating alone is not an enjoyable outing. If you are related to someone, you are somebody. If you are not related to anyone, you are nobody. Everyone wants to be somebody. None of us wants to be nobody. This is the typhoon blowing within us.

Unemployment is a terrible experience for anyone. It is so because the unemployed is without the means to make a living (money). But actually the most devastating blow of unemployment is the knowledge that 'you are not needed'. You are not needed —this we cannot bear. This eventually will kill us. We want to be needed. My name is Koyama. The name Koyama is quite important to me. Every time this name is mentioned I am interested to know why. When people speak my name I cannot be disinterested. Strange indeed! I do not

153

care much about someone else's name. When this particular one 'K-arachi, O-saka, Y-okohama, A-merica, M-alacca, A-merica'—as my secretary reads it˙ to the telegram office—is mentioned, the whole 'I' is there immediately. Why?

I want to be somebody. I want to be sure that I am needed. I do not want to hear that I am not needed. Is my name mentioned because 'I am needed' or because 'I am not needed'? *that* is what I want to know. 'Koyama, you are needed'—this makes me happy. 'Koyama, you are not needed'—this makes me unhappy. 'Koyama, you are needed by Koyama'—this does not make me happy. I want to be needed *by others*. I want to have others around me. I don't want to be ignored by others. This is the strong persistent wind—as strong as a typhoon—blowing within me.

You have a name. Of course you do. Your parents gave you your name. My wife and I have named our three children. *Naming* means 'I need you; you need me'. 'I need you; you need me' means *responsibility*. Responsibility is 'relatedness'. Irresponsibility is 'unrelatedness'. When my wife and I named our children we became responsible to them and they to us. Our relationship is 'we need each other' which is quite the opposite of the 'unemployment' situation. You call your friend by name. You call your wife by name. You call your teacher by name. You call your pet by name. Some people give names to fish in a family aquarium and call them by various names. To call someone by name means 'I need you; you need me'.

154

Where there is this relationship, there is *peace*.

This 'I need you; you need me' is the life-beat of our inner wind, that is, the human spirit. This is the powerful wind which makes our life meaningful. If this inner wind stops blowing or if this inner wind is confronted by continuous frustration, our life becomes uninteresting, uncreative and it degenerates. This inner wind ('spirit-typhoon') is actually much stronger than a typhoon that hits Hong Kong. A typhoon blows fiercely against an advertisement which says: 'Bookstore'. At the same time I notice another typhoon blowing within me which says 'That is a book shop. But look at me too, my name is Koyama. Please do not ignore me. I need you. You need me'.

floating restaurant meditation

Tao Fong Shan Christian Study Centre is located on a hill in Shatin, New Territories, Hong Kong. It was established about forty years ago by Dr. Karl Ludvig Reichelt with the purpose of facilitating Christian dialogue with the Chinese Buddhists. Shatin is a small but bustling town, but high on a hill the Study Centre is surrounded by pine trees and refreshing breezes blow in from the sea. In the evening you can watch the sparkling lights of Shatin by the water of the inlet between the hills. A floating restaurant on the water is colourfully illuminated. Thousands of lights placed in lines trace the contours of the building. An expensive electricity bill no doubt!

The illuminated straight horizontal lines do not blend with the background of the evening hills. Brightly lit straight lines look attractive but they make a disturbing contrast to nature's whispering and meditative lines. Dusk is a time for meditation and reflection on what we are, our relationship to the nature that embraces us. In the mysterious dusk everything gives us the impression of vertical-curve lines. Hills are a playful combination of vertical and curved lines. I recognize far away sampans on the water. They are rocking on the water. Smoke curls upwards from chimneys when evening meals are being prepared. It ascends in natural curves. I notice here and there bamboo groves where the spirits love to dwell, they are full of graceful vertical-curved lines. Artificial straight horizontal lines (aggressively illuminated!) disrupt the mood of meditation.

I want to look at hills, sampans, smoke and bamboo groves undisturbed, since I fail to spend my time with them. Perhaps I feel guilty because I spend so much of my time and energy in the world symbolized by 'illuminated horizontal lines'—the *world we make*. Deep in my soul I must be missing the *nature that is given to us* and surrounds us. As I watched the attractively illuminated contours of the restaurant against the background of the eternal hills I felt that I was suspended between the world we make and the nature we have not made. With the former I felt familiar and with the latter I felt unfamiliar! That alarmed me. But at the same time I felt nervous with the former and relaxed with the latter. It was a strange—but pleasant!—feeling of confusion.

I began to ask myself a difficult question: 'To which do I belong?'—the world we make or the nature we have not made? What is the relationship between civilization ('illuminated horizontal lines') and nature (hills and water)? How, in my spiritual life, can I arrange harmoniously the two kinds of lines—

157

straight-horizontal and vertical curve—so that I can live a meaningful life? I regretted asking such a question. Why should I ask such a nervous and unclear (ambiguous) question when I am supposed to be peaceful with the eternal hills in the mysterious dusk? But those 'illuminated horizontal lines'—they are still there! They do not disappear! They are forcing me to ask this question!

Chronologically speaking, of course, the hills and water (nature) came before 'illuminated horizontal lines' (civilization). This simple obvious observation made me happy. It means to me that I am rooted deeply in nature. This is a comforting thought, '...you return to the ground, for out of it you were taken; you are dust and to dust you shall return' (Genesis 3:19). This speaks of the truth, how deeply man is rooted in nature. I am glad that I am not as deeply rooted in civilization (from 'horizontal line' to 'illuminated horizontal line' to 'supersonic streak in the high sky') as I am rooted in nature. I felt that the hills spoke to me far more deeply than the illuminated horizontal lines. I wished that the floating restaurant did not exist there at all!

But what kind of life do I have if it is all 'hills and water' and no 'illuminated horizontal lines'? Look at the sampans in the distance! Are they not part of 'illuminated horizontal lines' since they are manmade (the world we make)? They are a vital part of man's civilization. How about the white smoke ascending slowly from the kitchens? Isn't that part of 'illuminated horizontal lines' (the world we make)? Isn't cooking with fire the beginning of hu-

158

man civilization? How about these winding roads and steps that I enjoy walking up to this Study Centre? Aren't roads and steps a fundamental part of human civilization? The Bible does not say '...you return to the "illuminated horizontal lines", for out of it you were taken; you "illuminated horizontal lines" to "illuminated horizontal lines" you shall return'. Yet I cannot live this life apart from human civilization (what man has made and is making). I wished that the floating restaurant was much bigger and dominated the entire scenery!

> When God began to create the heaven and the earth—the earth being unformed and void, with darkness over the surface of the deep and a wind from God sweeping over the water—God said, 'Let there be light'; and there was light. God saw how good the light was, and God separated the light from the darkness. God called the light Day, and the darkness He called Night, And there was evening and there was morning, a first day. Genesis 1:1-5

The Biblical affirmation is that it is God who created 'heaven and the earth' and not the other way around. This is simple and forceful truth. It is the truth that has a life-giving message for us today. Yet, it is the truth at which we stumble. We want the opening passage of the Bible to read: 'When the heaven and the earth began to create God, ...' If God derives from heaven and earth, he is a 'nature-god'. Then when we meditate upon hills and water we meditate upon God himself since He came from them. This would be an easy arrangement for all of us. The Bible rejects such an easygoing attractive theology.

God creates the heaven and the earth. He works on them. God, the Creator, means that he is not lazy.

159

'My father is working still, and I am working' (John 5:17). God works. God makes God's civilization. He does so making light (illumination in the dark!) The Bible is the Book of the Action of God. When God says 'I AM' it means 'I DO' (Exodus 3:13-15). The Biblical God is a Civilizer. The main constructor of God's civilization is Jesus Christ. The mind of Jesus Christ is the mind of God's civilization on earth.

> Have this mind among yourselves, which you have in Christ Jesus, who, though he was in the form of God, did not count equality·with God a thing to be grasped, but emptied himself, taking the form of a servant, being born in the likeness of man. And being found in human form he humbled himself and became obedient unto death, even death on a cross. Therefore God has highly exalted him and bestowed on him the name which is above every name, that at the name of Jesus every knee should bow, in heaven and on earth and under the earth. Philippians 2:4-11

Human civilization is a blessing to mankind as long as it is guided by the spirit of God's civilization. There is nothing wrong with building buildings, bridges, underground railways, airports (which are all symbolized by the 'illuminated horizontal line' of the Shatin floating restaurant) as long as they are guided by the mind of God's civilization among men.

Nuclear power is an unprecedented blessing for human civilization if it is used by the mind of God's civilization. All giant strides in transport are again a blessing to mankind if used by the mind of God's civilization. But when 'planes carry nuclear bombs and drop them on human beings, then, the whole human civilization suffers.

160

God is not against 'hills and water' (nature). He is not against 'illuminated horizontal lines' (human civilization). God is not against 'sampans and smoke' (man using technology). God is not against 'straight-horizontal lines' and 'vertical-curve lines' (two kinds of activities of human minds). God blesses them all. 'What God has cleansed you must not call common' (Acts 11:9).

> I lift up my eyes to the hills. From whence does my help come? My help comes from the Lord, who made heaven and earth. Psalm 121:1

I look out at the town of Shatin in the dusk. From whence does my help come? My help does not come from 'hills and water', 'illuminated horizontal lines', 'sampans and smoke', 'straight-horizontal lines and vertical-curve lines'. My help comes from the Lord who blesses *them all* through his holy intention of achieving civilization on earth in Jesus Christ. 'Thy will be done in earth as it is in heaven.'

i love the hong kong ferry

I love the Hong Kong-Kowloon ferry. What a refreshing ten minutes! After bustling about the congested hot streets you find yourself on the magnificent blue water. The air smells different. It is no longer petrol-fume air but sea air, the life-giving ozone-full air, the air that has kept all living creatures alive for millions and millions of years! This must be the air dinosaurs breathed, I tell myself.

Way out in the water you can see both the Kowloon side and the Hong Kong side. I tell myself 'Let's forget about land'. Scientists tell us that life originated in the water and not on the land. Water is our first home. Forget about land! Look at both sides—Kowloon and Hong Kong—are they not full of human toil, sweat and struggle? For ten minutes breathe ozone-full air to the full and think about dinosaurs! I paid twenty cents (first class Star Ferry) to get on this ferry, I might as well make the most of it!

Look into the distance. Dear friends, that is important. In our busy Hong Kong life we seldom look into the distance. We are all busy near-sighted people. We are like owls in the daytime. Our sight reaches only those things which are right in front of us. We want to have happiness in front of us, instant happiness, not long-distance happiness. We want to have money in front of us, instant money, not long-distance money. We have to have education in front of us, instant education, not long-distance education. We want to have a wife in front of us, instant wife, not a long-distance wife. Our life becomes instant life, travelling from one instant gain to one more instant gain and from one instant loss to one more instant loss. From instant joy to instant sorrow we travel. From instant life to instant death we go. But we are not supposed to live 'instantly'. While you are on the ferry, look into the distance.

Think of a long-distance style of life. You know about hairstyles. There are many hairstyles. Some you like, some you do not like. I am suggesting that we, today, need a long-distance style of life. A life style which may not be as magnificent as sparkling fireworks but which endures and deepens its genuine human quality. Such a life style, the life style which looks into the distance from time to time and navigates its course, is the kind of life style I think about on the ferry. I look into the distance. As I do this an ancient Greek wise man, Socrates, whispers to me 'unexamined life is not worth living'. I look into the distance again. Beautiful!

Look at the water, dear friends, that is important. Water, blue water, calm water, choppy water, angry water. There is infinitely more here than in your washbasin at home. More water than your bath can hold! Plenty of water. When we were in the womb we floated in the safety and comfort of water. Our life received initial nourishment through a mother's mild, sweet, life-giving water. We need water to drink, to bathe and to wash. Without water we cannot stay alive. Water is vital. Our life hangs on water, not petrol or oil. Yet it is so plentifully available. You are now sailing over the water, the life-giving water.

I remember two things: the safety and comfort of a mother's womb and the plentifulness of God, the Creator. Security and plentifulness— aren't these the two most needed things we yearn for? As I watch the water from the ferry deck I meditate on these two things. And every time I find something new in the water. I love the Hong Kong ferry.

coughing gods

And the soldiers led him away inside the palace (that is, the
praetorium); and they called together the whole battalion.
And they clothed him in a purple cloak, and plaiting a crown
of thorns they put it on him. And they began to salute him,
'Hail, King of the Jews!' And they struck his head with a reed,
and spat upon him, and they knelt down in homage to him.
And when they had mocked him, they stripped him of the
purple cloak, and put his own clothes on him. And they led
him out to crucify him. ...And those who passed by derided
him, wagging their heads, and saying, 'Aha! You who would
destroy the temple and build it in three days, save yourself,
and come down from the cross!' So also the chief priests
mocked him to one another with the scribes saying, 'He saved
others; he cannot save himself. Let the Christ, the King of
Israel, come down now from the cross, that we may see and
believe.' Those who were crucified with him also reviled him.
Mark 15:16-20

One evening I visited an old Chinese temple on
Philip Street. It was celebrating an occasion related
to the Chinese New Year. This temple must be as
old as Singapore. As I neared Philip Street the
strong smell of burning joss-sticks was already in
the air. People were streaming into this tiny temple
with lanterns and joss-sticks in their hands. An
ever-increasing number of people were milling
around a narrow stone gate (the only way into the
inner yard of the temple) with lighted lanterns and

joss-sticks in their hands. Coming from Tokyo I am used to moving among a crowd, but I am not used to a crowd carrying burning joss-sticks. I let myself be swept into the swirl of violent current, as it were, and it took me into the inner yard. This too was full of people (all Chinese)—some squatting and others standing, burning joss-sticks on the stone floor. The lovely moonlit sky was smoky (and polluted!) by the burning of thousands of cheap joss-sticks. As I coughed I said to myself, the moon must be coughing too.

The innermost section of the temple (about five square metres) was absolutely packed with people, all pushing their way towards the central bowl. There was a counter selling 'luck' papers and money was pouring in. At the centre table stood two men in every-day clothes who from time to time shouted something at the people. They were not dressed like priests, but they might have been performing some kind of priestly functions—although they looked to me more like bargain salesmen. Tears came to my eyes, not because of inspiration, but because of the smoke from the joss-sticks that thickly enveloped this inner temple. I noticed that others were 'crying' too. A number of women were, with unperturbed devotion, kneeling and shaking lucky sticks. They bowed and cried again and again as though they were enraptured. My eyes began to hurt. My lungs began to protest. Whatever god it was, it must have been coughing and crying too.

I was close enough to the people to feel their en-

167

thusiasm. I felt as if I was one of them. And I began to wonder about the kinds of human stories each one of them must have experienced. It must be an important community function of fellowship for these people to congregate at this temple once a year at the New Year. I did not feel that they were very different from me. On this particular night I found myself pondering on the idea of 'luck-bringing religion' and I have been thinking about it since. It is my problem and perhaps it is their problem too.

The 'luck-bringing god' is perhaps the most popular god. Forty miles outside Tokyo there is a 'luck-bringing-god' temple called *Narita-San*. All the year round, year in and year out this temple sells various 'protection oracles' against evil spirits, traffic accidents, sickness; and 'luck words' which read 'your business will grow and you will make more and more money and your wife will always be beautiful!' *Narita-San*, of course, makes a fantastic income! As I see it *Narita-San* is one of the most successful businesses in operation. Print some lucky words on the fast-running printing press and all this printed matter will be turned into cash! And people buy them without bargaining. Their money is taken away and yet they are grateful! How about that! Do you know a better business?

There are perhaps two kinds of religion: 'luck-bringing religion' and 'not-luck-bringing religion'. The former is popular but the latter is not. The human mind is very interested in 'luck-bringing religion' and we are constantly making all kinds of

168

'luck-bringing gods'. Actually we are not interested in 'gods'. We are interested in what they bring. So 'gods' were coughing in the polluted air that night, but that did not matter to the people. In most cases 'luck' means 'money'. 'Luck-bringing religion' then means 'money-bringing religion'. They were interested in what the gods bring (money) this year of the Tiger. We perform such 'religious operations' with great concentration, dedication and imagination.

Thick smoke from the joss-sticks

We all love 'luck-bringing religion' who doesn't?

I wonder if this tremendous enthusiasm for 'luck-bringing religion' is the source from which all kinds of superstition have come. The distinction between superstition and religion is not easy to make. Unfortunately religious practices often become superstitious practices. Perhaps no religion is free from this as long as it is believed by us, since we are incorrigibly interested in 'luck-(or money-)bringing religion'. We are capable of making a superstition

169

out of Christianity. This is a subject we must think about carefully. This is an extremely subtle subject. To put this in theological language: 'man is capable of making a law out of the Gospel'. This basic distortion of making the Gospel into Law is the tragic source from which all superstition comes. Superstition is a practice which is guided by the spirit which says, 'I am interested in what the gods bring to me!'

The Biblical faith is not a 'luck-bringing religion'. It rejects the commercial position (*theological pious commercialism*) that 'I believe in God because if I believe in God I will have good luck'. This is tantamount to saying: 'You know I am not interested in God. I am not interested in Jesus Christ. Actually I do not care about the Father, Son and Holy Spirit. But I am interested in what God in Christ brings to me!' If we do this, are we not *using* God for our gain? Are we not treating our God in the same way as the people in the old Chinese temple in Philip Street treat the coughing god? 'Good luck' may come to Christians. 'Good luck' may *not* come to Christians. 'Good luck' is not a central issue. The Apostles' Creed says: 'I believe in God the Father Almighty, the Maker of Heaven and Earth...' *I believe in God.* It does not say: 'I believe in what God brings to me if I believe in God'. Do you like to be loved by someone because of *what you are* or *what you have*? Which? But as soon as I write this I feel that I am speaking very arrogantly. Do I know the distinction between 'using God' and 'worshipping God'? Do I use him? Yes. I do! Help my unbelief.

170

'Those who passed by derided him, wagging their heads...', 'He saved others; he cannot save himself...' True, he saved others. But he did not save himself. He was crucified. Why did he not save himself?

By giving his own life—*not something else*—Jesus Christ spoke and came to us. Not by giving his 'money', 'luck' and 'something he brings', but by giving *himself* he came to us. This giving himself is called *Love* in the New Testament. Love is abundant in giving. Love is free. Love is graceful. Love rejects 'commercial transactions'. Note what the chief priest and scribes said: 'Let the Christ, the King of Israel, come down from the cross, that we may see and believe'. This is based upon their commercial-transaction theology. Nailed down he destroys the source of superstition. On the cross Love triumphs.

Love then rejects 'religious commercialism'. Love judges the coughing god and his people. By judging them, it gives them life. Human life must not run on the principle of commercialism. It must be run by the power of self-giving Love.

the rev'd john wesley

A Methodist is one who has the love of God shed abroad in his heart by the Holy Ghost given unto him. One who loves the Lord his God with all his heart and soul and mind and strength. He rejoices evermore, prays without ceasing, and in everything gives thanks. His heart is full of love to all mankind and is purified from envy, wrath, malice, and every unkind affection. His one desire and the one design of his life is not to do his own will but the will of Him that sent him. He keeps all God's commandments from the least to the greatest. He follows not the customs of the world, for vice does not lose its nature by becoming fashionable. He cannot join in any diversion that has the least tendency to evil. He cannot speak evil of his neighbour any more than he can lie. He cannot utter unkind or evil words. He does good unto all men, unto neighbours, strangers, friends and enemies. These are the principles and practices of our communion. These are the marks of a true Methodist. By these alone do Methodists desire to be distinguished from all other men.

(John Wesley)

Dear John Wesley,

Millions of people today call themselves Methodists. There are Methodist schools, Methodist hospitals, Methodist churches and The World Methodist Council. The sun never sets on Methodists! This is, humanly speaking, a great tribute to you.

You were a Christian. This is the basic thing to be said about you. Your life was changed when the living Christ touched you. One of the most amazing careers in the history of the Christian church began at Aldersgate when you, an Anglican, listened to Luther's preface to the *Commentary on Romans* in 1738. What you have written in your journal has been read by millions: 'About a quarter before nine, while he (Luther) was describing the change which God works in the heart through faith in Christ, I felt my heart strangely warmed. I felt I did trust in Christ, Christ alone, for salvation; and an assurance was given me that he had taken away my sins, even mine, and saved me from the law of sin and death'.

I see here expressed the heart of Protestantism—salvation by faith alone! 'I felt I did trust in Christ, Christ alone, for salvation!' You are a 'Christ-alone truster'. Christ liberated you! You resolved to think of nothing but Jesus Christ—Christ nailed to the cross! (I Corinthians 2:2). This is the conviction that gave more than all the energy you needed for your ministry.

Some two hundred and thirty years after Aldersgate, people in Singapore still read your description of what 'A Methodist is...' and I must say (who am I to speak like this to you—I trust you will pardon me) that probably your description will be only superficially understood. Methodists will read it through in some thirty seconds and still think they are Methodists. What you have written points to a tremendous height of sanctified life. You are liter-

173

ally requiring your people to practise the 'Sermon on the Mount'. My immediate reaction to your definition of what a Methodist is: Then there are only two Methodists in the whole world, Jesus Christ and John Wesley! I do not expect to see this high quality of Christian life in the house of Methodist Bishops.

Well, I am puzzled by your description of a Methodist. You seem to place emphasis on what a Methodist is and what a Methodist does. Surely a Methodist is, in the first place, in the most fundamental sense, a Christian, a 'Christ-alone truster'. Liberated by Christ! (Galatians 3:13). The Christian faith is emphasis on Jesus Christ. Who he was and who he is, what he did and what he does (Colossians 1:15-20) must precede who we are and what we are. 'But God shows his love for us in that while we were yet sinners Christ died for us' (Romans 5:8). Basically a Methodist is a person who is a 'Christ-alone truster' since He alone is the Liberator. This must be the essential thing to be said about a Methodist, since it is exactly the essential thing to be said about a Christian. The fundamental mark of a Methodist and of a Christian must be identical otherwise there arises the dangerous possibility of a person's being Methodist but not Christian.

All Christians are, in this most basic sense, Methodists. All Methodists are Methodists secondarily, not primarily. Would you agree that if being a Methodist becomes a matter of primary distinction, then an 'I-belong-to-Wesley' will take place? Paul's

174

rebuke sings out: 'Is Christ divided? Was Paul crucified for you? Or were you baptized in the name of Paul?' (I Corinthians 1:13). I belong to Wesley?

Why did you say 'these are the marks of a true Methodist'? Is a true Methodist different from a true Christian? Does what makes a true Christian automatically make a man a true Methodist? You may say that Methodists are those who have achieved a special degree of sanctified living. Can anyone achieve such high standards? Is 'to be a Methodist' a real possibility? I wonder how many of those millions can truly call themselves Methodists.

Sincerely yours,

god and theology, wife and wife-ology

There is a difference between God and theology. This is as obvious as the difference between wife and wife-ology. (If they were the same it would be much easier to handle!) The famous John 3:16 does not say 'For theology so loved the world that he gave his only Son...' God can neither be equated with theology nor contained in theology. The New Testament speaks about 'The Kingdom of God' and not 'kingdom of theology'. There is the sovereign God but there cannot be the sovereign theology, no matter how great. All theologies are very humble human attempts to say something about God because God has first spoken to us. God first loved us (I John 4:19). Theology does not walk on the street any more than wife-ology does. Man who engages in theology walks. He becomes a 'man of theology' (sociologically called theologian). When God comes to him he finds himself saying what the young Jeremiah said: 'Ah, Lord God! Behold, I do not know how to speak, for I am only a youth' (Jeremiah 1:6). This is the genuine mark of those who engage in theology. In theology we do not know how to speak!

f.p.c. versus god

We often hear that 'we are scientific and technological men'. God does not give us a 'fresh breeze
of cool air' but an air-conditioner does. God does
not heal the sick but medical doctors do. While we
have a tremendous population problem God is silent. In our day fish-understanding is looked upon
as a more worthy enterprise than 'nebulous' 'God
understanding'. Fish 'can be turned into FPC: fish
protein concentrate, by grinding up almost all the
fish into flour. FPC can be added to cereals, used
with ordinary flour when making bread, and mixed
with almost any type of food. FPC is eighty-five
per cent protein. A beef steak is a mere twenty-
five per cent protein.' (*The World of Tomorrow* by
K.K. Goldstein, p.16) The world population is ex-
ploding! Fish-understanding can give us the tremendous resource in protein (our hope is in marine protein!) but God-understanding can produce neither
protein nor vitamins! In the same vein, don't we
often hear that we are today living the life of scientific and technological man? Here is a 'confession of faith': there is not much room left for God.
Every discovery, application, invention will dis-

177

credit God and credit man. The oxcart gave God plenty of room; the motorcar took some of this room away; the aeroplane took even more space and the supersonic jet just about squeezed God out. Less mystery, less God. God's unemployment is right around the corner. At least he should be retired with a good pension and rest in quiet heaven. We will not 'cry unto Thee'. We will cry unto science and technology which have taken the place of God. We shall not say 'Our Father which art in heaven', but 'our technology on earth'. Science and technology are our messiah. The sooner we realize this the better.

Can God survive? I don't think he will. I mean this kind of God who is increasingly edged out by human progress. He is pretty dead in the minds of men already. But the unemployment or death of this kind of God need not alarm us. He is like a father who appears on the scene only when he is called on to settle a dispute among his children. He straightens things out. Population explosion! He is called on! He takes a definite line of action—he straightens it out. He is a 'straightener'. Like Mary Poppins who straightens up the children's room with the snap of a finger. This kind of God will rightly be replaced by science and technology. A God who is pushed out by technology, let him be pushed out. This God is controlled by technology, and is a servant to man's convenience and comfort.

Is there then a different kind of God? Yes. He is the God who does not speak to technology and science, but to man who uses technology and science. He speaks to everyone (men and women, educated or uneducated—whether or not they are interested in astrology as I have witnessed in the back streets of Tokyo). He says to us 'man (remember God is addressing man) cannot live on bread (all the benefits of science and technology) alone, but lives by every word that comes from the mouth of the Lord' (Deuteronomy 8:3). The word of the Lord is that man must use and control technology. When technology uses man, man ceases to be man. 'Fill the earth and subdue it' (Genesis 1:28), but don't let the earth and all its power and influence subdue man. As technology increases its influence so man's need for the word of God becomes greater.

personal freedom — two billion times

We hear about two billion people.

'By "two billion" I mean', writes Dr. Donald McGavran, 'those multitudes of men and women who do not know Jesus Christ as Lord and Saviour. They are found in all six continents, but by far the largest numbers are in Asia, Africa and Latin America. In these lands, blocks of humanity are found (numbering tens of thousands and sometimes millions in each block) in the midst of which can be found no church, no Bible and no Christian. In the whole world, only about one billion call themselves "Christians". Two billion have never heard His name effectively.' *Church Growth Bulletin*, July 1971 Christians must bring 'His name effectively' to these 'two billion untouched people'.

What a gigantic responsibility! What a tremendous assignment! It is a difficult task—a task which can never be performed without the grace of God!— even to speak 'five intelligible words' about Jesus Christ to five persons (I Corinthians 14:19). Now we are confronted by two billion people!

Quite obviously, I cannot evangelize two billion alone. I understand that one billion Christians are responsible for this task. One billion Christians! Two billion non-Christians! The idea is simple, but what it implies is too vast for me—I have lived only a mere forty years or so of life—to appreciate its horizon and substance. Demographers project that our planet will have a population of thirty billion by 2050! I try, within my feeble and tiny framework of faith and theology, to meditate on the destiny of two billion. I try, but I must confess I am confused every time by the sheer immensity and ambiguity of the thought. Am I unbelieving? Am I making God 'small' as though He does not know how to handle two billion? After all, I must not forget that we have one billion Christians to do the job? Don't I understand or am I disobedient to the command of the risen Lord: 'Go forth therefore and make all nations my disciples...' (Matthew 29:18-20).

I am delighted to know that one light year is 5.88 billion miles and that the Milky Way from one end to the other is a distance of one hundred thousand light years. In 1970 Japanese exports to South East Asia totalled 7.5 billion pounds. In 1970-71 India received 33 million pounds of aid from West Germany. In 1970 the G.N.P. of Pakistan was 15 billion pounds. These figures, even though they are not ordinary numbers, I can handle in my everyday life, they speak to me directly. But when we speak of human beings in astronomical numbers, it does not and cannot speak to me directly. It takes a lot of thinking to grasp the substance of it. The idea of two billion pounds—although I shall never possess it—does not confuse me. I think it must be due to the fact that I am convinced somewhere in the depth of my quality of 'being human' that I, the human being, am of greater value than even two billion pounds. The idea of two billion people comes to me in a completely different way. Immediately I sense that I cannot tame them, I cannot control them, I cannot possess them. They do not come, in any sense, under my command or wish. Two billion people means personal freedom two billion times, human dignity two billion times, mystery of the image of God two billion times, personal history two billion times, two billion ways to use money and two billion ways to experience life. There is a sacred dimension in man which defies and rejects being numbered. It involves a very dangerous simplification to speak of one billion and two billion in terms of evangelism.

'Go forth!' Right. But how are we going forth? With a *crusading mind* as though the whole strategy of God's salvation of man is dependent upon man's performance? Or with a *crucified mind* that *all* is in God's hands and all that is required of us is 'to take up the cross and follow him' without counting numbers? And how can we evangelize people with the message of the crucified One unless it is communicated by the crucified mind? Joachim Jeremias, a professor of New Testament theology, in his critical study of the New Testament, has this to say:

What is significant for the missionary task is the realization to which we have been brought, that it is firmly rooted in God's redemptive activity. In Jesus' sayings about the Gentiles we find an unparallelled insistence on humility. Man can do nothing. It is not our preaching that brings the ingathering of the Gentiles. *Even Jesus himself did not make the world Christian, but he died on the Cross.* God alone does it all. The fundamental note and inmost core of the message of Jesus, resounding in all his sayings about the Gentiles is confidence in the reality of God and the vastness of his mercy.

(Jesus' Promise to the Nations, p.74)

God calls us in His sovereign freedom to His work. It is His job to count numbers since He is able to call each of us by name (Isaiah 40:26; John 10:3). 'He calls us'—is the mystery of His amazing generosity (Matthew 20:1-16). Is this 'His work' equivalent with evangelization of two billion as we con-- ceive it? Or is it something more? Are we Christians to discharge the mission as we define it or as God defines it? Is our understanding always identical with God's understanding? Does God who came to us in Jesus Christ speak of the urgency of mission in terms of two billion people? Is our sense of urgency identical? Is God as impatient with history as we are? In what way does God speak to two billion? Does he wish for church growth along the same lines as we do?

For in making all mankind prisoners to disobedience, God's purpose was to show mercy to all mankind.

O depth of wealth, wisdom, and knowledge in God! How unsearchable his judgments, how untraceable his ways! Who knows the mind of the Lord? Who has been his counsellor? Who has ever made a gift to him, to receive a gift in return? Source, Guide and Goal of all that is—to him be the glory for ever! Amen. Romans 11:32-36

183

japan expo '70

One of the several critical issues which confronted the Christian Church in Japan in 1970 was this: 'Should Japanese Christians *support* or *oppose* the Christian Pavilion in Expo '70 to be held in Osaka?' Perhaps this may sound strange to many of us. What is wrong with having a Christian Pavilion in the compound of Expo '70? There were two opposing views within the Christian Church which clashed violently during the two years prior to the event. The debate had become so critical in the life of the United Church of Christ in Japan that an Extraordinary Assembly (the second of its kind in twenty-eight years) was called in November 1969 to discuss this specific issue. The reasons for support or objection were complicated. They were rooted in political, social, economic, theological and missiological concerns. Both sides were dead serious and extremely vocal about their own position. Here was a great contemporary theological debate!

Opposition: Expo '70 is a 'Festival of Baal' in which the might of capitalist exploitation will glory itself.

It is a 'Big Yes!' to materialistic prosperity. It will supply an immense amount of 'tranquilizing pills' to the conscience of the millions of people about 'these least ones'. It is a sheer celebration of man's technological advances and prosperity! The Church cannot engage in genuine evangelism within the compound of the 'cult of prosperity worship'. *Because of this*, we are against the Christian Pavilion at Expo '70.

Support: We are not so naive as to say that Expo '70 does not contain ugly human pride and exploitation. There is human darkness in it. But we want to support the building of the Christian Pavilion right in the compound of what the opposition calls 'Festival of Baal'. If Expo '70 is so bad and wicked, doesn't it need, all the more, the presence of Jesus Christ? 'And the Word became flesh and dwelt among us.' More than that, we must affirm that Jesus Christ will surely be there at Expo '70! He knows more than any of us how "dirty" Expo '70 is. In spite of that, He will be present there! The Christian Pavilion is the symbol of His presence in the midst of today's world. There will be seventy million visitors at Expo '70 (according to computer forecasts). These people will walk through the U.S. Pavilion, the Canadian Pavilion, the Thai Pavilion and the Singapore Pavilion, and so on. Now they come to the Christian Pavilion which will ask them 'theological questions' about these technological advancements and ultra-modern life styles projected. It will ask people this: should we be simply so intoxicated by man's great achievements? Aren't there some very crucial issues hidden in

185

'scientific blessings' which escape our attention? What is the relationship between 'progress' and 'human happiness'? The Christian Pavilion will make people 'come to their senses' (Luke 15:17). Furthermore, think of seventy million! What a magnificent occasion for evangelism this is! In spite of all dilemmas and human darkness the Church must build and support the Christian Pavilion at Expo '70 as the sign of the presence of the Incarnate Son of God in the world today.

Thus there were two groups: (1) the 'because of' group (opposition), and (2) the 'in spite of' group (support). The former insisted on 'prophetic distance', the latter 'prophetic involvement'. *Both* theologically grounded 'distance' and 'involvement' revolved around the Christian Pavilion at Expo '70. Isn't it true that at clashing points of 'because of' and 'in spite of', we should and we can pray together 'Thy will be done on earth as it is in heaven'?

the moon and irresponsibility

In the Spring, cherry blossom,
in the summer the cuckoo.
In the Autumn the moon, and in
Winter the snow, clear, cold.
                    Priest Dogan (1200-1253)

This well-known Japanese medieval poem speaks deeply to the Japanese mind. Japan is blessed with the changing seasons which bring out the amazing beauty of nature with an ever-refreshing touch. Winter is not too severe to endure. Summer is not too hot to bear. Moderate yet distinctive turns of the season make man's emotions and thoughts rich and perceptive. Japanese people are like any other people who have lived intimately with mother nature. The Japanese novelist Mr. Kawabata, the winner of the 1968 Nobel Prize for literature, says that they learned to experience deep human feeling in communion with 'snow, moon, cherries in bloom'.

As a Japanese gazes at the autumn moon, he feels the philosophy of nothingness gradually permeating his soul and mood. The world is full of strife,

187

injustice, suffering. But as I meditate on them in the moonlight all becomes 'quiet and clear' (nothingness) as the moon over the mountain.

The sentiment of aesthetic nothingness is deeply embedded in the soul of each Japanese even in today's highly industrialized society. It is different from the West's concept of 'nothingness'. In the Western mentality, the highest value, God, is defined as an opposite of 'nothingness'. God is Being. Nothingness then means a threat to the world which is created and sustained by *God who is*. In the tradition where the Christian understanding of God the Creator forms a cultural undercurrent, an aesthetic sentiment of nothingness cannot become as vocal and as unrestrained as it is in Japanese life. I am not denying the possibility of aesthetic appreciation of nothingness in the West. I am saying it is checked one way or another by the concept of God and His world. In Japan nature (snow, blossom, moon in particular) invites one to see oneself in the ultimately 'quiet and clear' light of the moon. What the moon represents to the Japanese soul is an instant experience of transcendence. It is instant in the sense that it is basically aesthetic and not ethical. The ethical automatically becomes silent. It is quite out of tune to discuss, or even meditate on ethical issues (social justice, political organization, problems of modernization, ecology, pollution, international power struggles, nuclear balances of terror) while you are looking at the moon. You meditate on the transitoriness of your life and forget all modern headaches.

When we see the beauty of the snow, when we see the beauty of the full moon, when we see the beauty of the cherries in bloom, when in short we brush against and are awakened by the beauty of the four seasons, it is then that we think most of those close to us, and want them to share the pleasure. The excitement of beauty calls forth strong fellow feelings, yearnings for companionship, and the word 'comrade' can be taken to mean 'human being'. The snow, the moon, the blossoms, words expressive of the seasons as they move into another, include in the Japanese tradition the beauty of mountains and rivers, grasses and trees, of all the myriad manifestations of nature, of human feelings as well. That spirit, that feeling for one's comrades in the snow, the moonlight, is also basic to the tea ceremony.

(*Japan the Beautiful and Myself*, A speech by Yasunari Kawabata on the occasion of his receiving the Nobel Prize 1968, pp.68-69)

It is increasingly difficult to enjoy the 'quiet and clear moon' in Japan, the land of chimneys and polluted air. A great majority of Japanese people today live under a roof twenty-four hours a day—in their home, in a train, a car or an office. Their contact with the moon is severely limited. Vast industrialization has minimized a people's (historic) contact with the moon. But the same feeling is there in busy modern Japanese souls! They can become

the coughing moon

instantly 'quiet and clear' in the autumn moon. In this sense Japanese people are unpredictable. There is this special character of Japanese spiritual transcendence. No doubt the moment is aesthetic and, let me say, irresponsible.

In August 1945 when Japan accepted 'unconditional surrender' to the Allied Forces, high-ranking military men committed suicide.

In another section of Tokyo the creator of the *kamikase* corps, Admiral Takijiro Onishi, lay mortally wounded by his own hand in his home. He sent for his associate and friend, Oshio Kodama, whose sword he had borrowed the night before. Kodama found Onishi still conscious, though he had slit his abdomen and stabbed himself in the chest and throat. He seized Kodama's hand. 'What I want to tell you is written in my will on the top of the desk. There's also a letter to my wife; she is in the country.' He smiled faintly, 'I thought your sword was sharper. It didn't cut very well.'

The weapon was on the floor, and Kodama picked it up. 'Your Excellency', he whispered, 'I will go with you.'

'*Bakayaro!*' Onishi shouted in a surprisingly strong voice. 'What would you gain by dying now? Instead—there is another letter on my desk. Take it to Atsugi Air Base at once and bring those headstrong men under control. That will do more good for Japan than dying here.' His forehead was cov-

190

ered with perspiration and he gasped for words. 'Many of the nationalists will rise up. Stop them!'

Kodama found the letter on the desk. In it the man who a few days before had pleaded with Admiral Toyoda and Foreign Minister Togo to sacrifice twenty million lives in a final defence of the homeland apologized for his failure to bring victory. He wanted the young people of Japan to find a moral in his death. 'To be reckless is only to aid the enemy. You must abide by the spirit of the Emperor's decision with utmost perseverance. Do not forget your rightful pride in being Japanese. You are the treasure of the nation. With all fervour of spirit of the Special Attackers, strive for the welfare of Japan and for peace throughout the world.'

Beside the letter was a *haiku*, Onishi's last poem:

> *Refreshed,*
> *I feel like the clear moon*
> *after a storm.*

The Rising Sun by John Toland, p.855

191